STAR WARS™

THE SKYWALKER SAGA

STAR WARS™

THE SKYWALKER SAGA

The *Star Wars* Skywalker saga, the three-trilogy, nine-film cycle has proven to be a timeless modern mythology, far exceeding being a mere staple of popular culture. Its icons are recognized all around the world and its story has been repeated on countless occasions, handed down from generation to generation.

The official magazine of the *Star Wars* franchise, *Star Wars Insider* (1994–present), was born of earlier fan-led endeavors: the newsletter *Bantha Tracks* (1978–1987) and the *Lucasfilm Fanclub Magazine* (1987–1994). What these three publications had in common was a desire to bring the very best of the galaxy far, far away to fans around the world, with exclusive interviews and rarely seen photographs, thrilling readers in those pre-internet days.

This volume contains interview material with the talented people who brought George Lucas' epic saga to life, taken from those long out-of-print periodicals. From the prequels to the original trilogy to the sequel trilogy, here are the members of the cast and crew of all nine films who were there, sharing their experiences on working on the greatest cinema saga of them all.

TITAN EDITORIAL
Editor Jonathan Wilkins
Managing Editor Martin Eden
Art Director Oz Browne
Senior Designer Andrew Leung
Proofreader Stephanie Hetherington
Assistant Editor Phoebe Hedges
Production Controller Caterina Falqui
Senior Production Controller Jackie Flook
Sales and Circulation Manager Steve Tothill
Marketing and Sales Coordinator George Wickenden
Marketing and Advertisement Assistant Lauren Noding
Publicist Imogen Harris
Acquisitions Editor Duncan Baizley
Publishing Director Ricky Claydon
Publishing Director John Dziewiatkowski
Operations Director Leigh Baulch
Publishers Nick Landau and Vivian Cheung

DISTRIBUTION
U.S. Newsstand: Total Publisher Services, Inc.
John Dziewiatkowski, 630-851-7683
U.S. Distribution: Ingrams Periodicals,
Curtis Circulation Company
U.K. Newsstand: Marketforce, 0203 787 9199
U.S./U.K. Direct Sales Market: Diamond Comic Distributors
For more info on advertising contact adinfo@titanemail.com

Contents © 2021 Lucasfilm Ltd. & TM. All Rights Reserved

First edition: May 2021

Star Wars: The Skywalker Saga The Official Movie Special is published by Titan Magazines, a division of Titan Publishing Group Limited, 144 Southwark Street, London, SE1 0UP

Printed in USA by Trans Con.

For sale in the U.S., Canada, U.K., and Eire

ISBN: 9781787734661

Titan Authorized User. TMN 14084

No part of this publication may be reproduced, stored in a retrival system, or transmitted, in any form or by any means, without the prior written permission of the publisher.

A CIP catalogue record for this title is available from the British Library.

10 9 8 7 6 5 4 3 2 1

LUCASFILM EDITORIAL
Senior Editor Brett Rector
Art Director Troy Alders
Creative Director Michael Siglain
Story Group Leland Chee, Pablo Hidalgo
Creative Art Manager Phil Szostak
Asset Management Chris Argyropoulos, Nicole LaCoursiere, Sarah Williams
Special Thanks: Lynne Hale, Christopher Troise, Eugene Paraszczuk

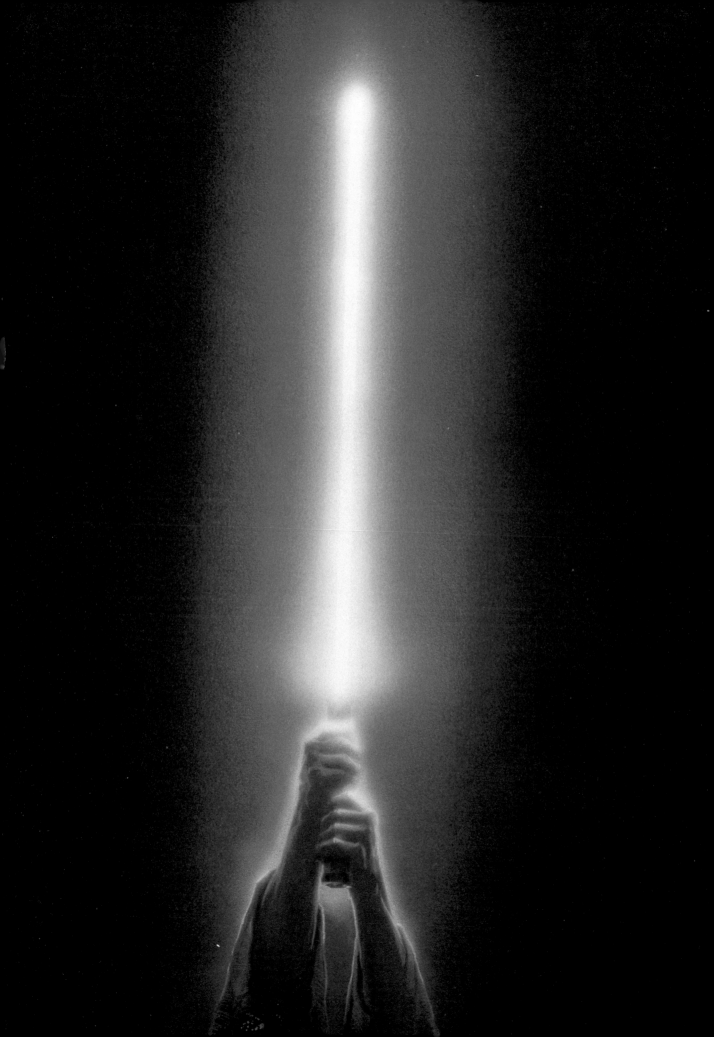

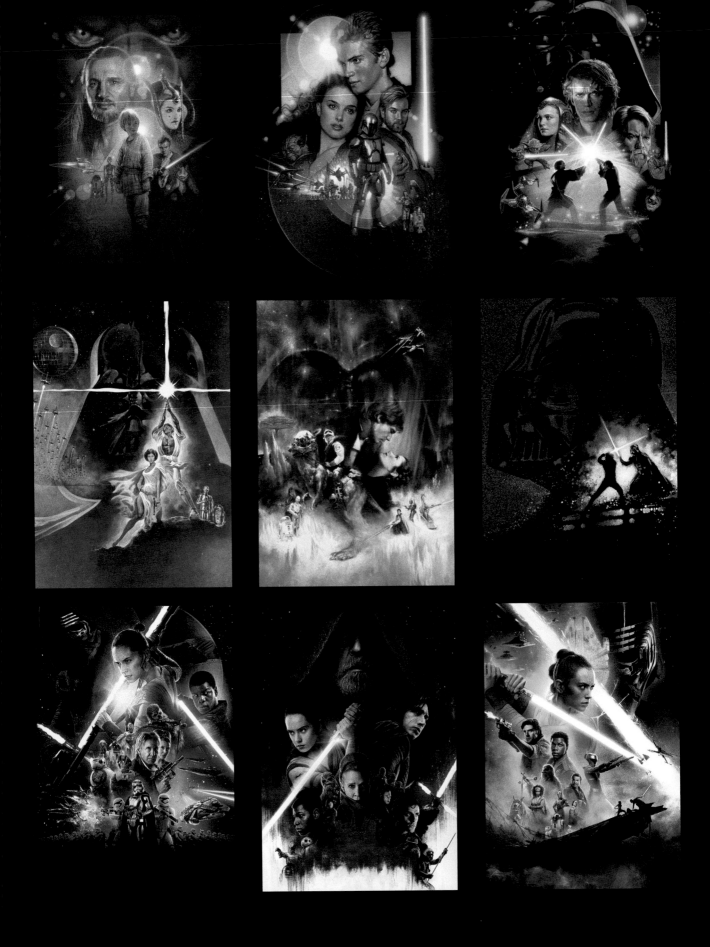

CONTENTS

THE PREQUEL TRILOGY

1999–2005

1 / Obi-Wan Kenobi (Ewan McGregor), Jake Lloyd (Anakin Skywalker), and Qui-Gon Jinn (Liam Neeson) face *The Phantom Menace* alongside saga veteran R2-D2. (Previous spread)

2 / The high octane podrace sequence picks up the pace.

3 / The Trade Federation make their prescence felt on Naboo.

4 / Second unit director Roger Christian consults with George Lucas on location in Tunisia.

In the late 1990s, George Lucas embarked on an epic journey to tell the story of how Anakin Skywalker turned to the dark side, how the galaxy fell under the evil Emperor's cruel Imperial dictatorship, and how the Jedi became, to quote Obi-Wan Kenobi, "all but extinct." Utilizing technology seemingly brought about by Lucas' own will to tell the story on his terms, the groundbreaking new trilogy took audiences back even earlier than the "long time ago" of the original trilogy.

George Lucas (Writer/Director): I had always intended to do Episodes I, II, and III. When I finished the first three, I decided I needed a hiatus. I'd worked on *Star Wars* for nine years and I was interested in doing other things.

Plus, the technology hadn't evolved enough for me to really do what I wanted to do. It's frustrating to work in a very limited palette. You might say that on the first three films I worked in a black and white palette but, with the second trilogy, I was able to add a lot more color. New special effects allow me to have Yoda walk. It allows me new alien characters, new droids, and a lot more varied vehicles than just spacecraft. From a director's point of view, it was hard on the earlier films because everybody's cemented in place. It's difficult to direct a scene when your actors can't move around.

Rick McCallum (Producer): The challenge is to make these new *Star Wars* films on time and on budget and with the highest

artistic commitment that we can make, and have them compete with all the other films Hollywood is producing.

George Lucas: The designers started working on the film the same time I started working on the script, which was two and a half years before filming began. For example, I needed designs for the speeders on Naboo that were reminiscent of the one that Luke was driving but that would fit better into a more Italian-looking setting. I was using a myriad of influences that would come from numerous places including art nouveau and Victorian versions of Italian Renaissance.

Doug Chiang (Design Director): I learned so much from George about film design rather than just

4 /

design. There are different concerns in film. George looks at the work, elaborates, and dismisses things in ten seconds. He doesn't want explanations when he reviews concepts—it just goes up on the board and it either reads or dies. It has to be bold or it doesn't work. The audience is not going to hear your explanation about why it's a good design or how it works.

George Lucas: I work in this great, odd genre that doesn't really exist. It's a mini-series done with feature length films, and it's not done as one unit. It's done over what will eventually be forty years. It will ultimately be twelve hours of just one story. It's broken into a bunch of pieces. But it's one book. Nobody has ever really done that. I'm doing very stylistic things, that are very musical in terms of how I

develop themes and repeat themes. I go over the same thing again and again in certain areas to echo what I have done before. It's like a symphony more than a movie. Some people may not understand what I'm doing. They think [*The Phantom Menace* is] just *Star Wars* with a shorter Luke Skywalker, but it is all done on purpose to create a certain feeling when you watch them all in order. Certain lines become more meaningful. It's going to change the first three movies rather dramatically. That's my whole reason for doing it; I like the idea that you can take something and look at it one way and then turn it around and, with more information, can look at things completely differently.

To tell the story, Lucas needed technology to take a major leap

ahead. As with the original trilogy, he was the man to give it the push it needed.

George Lucas: We were dependent on new technology to emerge during the production process. That scared a lot of people. We depended on our ability to come up with a lot of new ideas for things that don't exist. Industrial Light & Magic (ILM) spent nine months reinventing techniques. We had to write new software to achieve some of the things I wanted to do.

Rick McCallum: George thought that if he is doing these movies, why not do it right? He needed to be able to set up the tone, style, and look. I was thrilled when he agreed to direct. It really felt like ▶

5 /

he had never stopped directing. He has been directing this movie in his mind for nearly 20 years. He's just now showing the rest of us.

Jedi Master Qui-Gon Jinn was played by celebrated actor Liam Neeson, who led a cast of actors, some familiar, some making their motion picture debuts.

Liam Neeson (Qui-Gon Jinn): Qui-Gon is Alan Ladd in *Shane* (1953) crossed with Toshiro Mifune in *Seven Samurai* (1954) crossed with George Lucas. I always wanted to be a cowboy, and Jedi are like cowboys in space! George employs you because you are a good carpenter, actor, or designer. He lets you just get on with it. Eight times out of ten, George's direction will be "Speak a little bit faster on that line" or "When you turn, could you pick him up with your right hand instead of your left."

George Lucas: Liam Neeson is like Alec Guinness in the first movie. There isn't anybody else who has that sense of nobility and strength and calm. Jake Lloyd is a natural. He's bouncy and cheerful. He has to have the same kind of presence that a young Luke Skywalker has in the first film. Natalie Portman is perfect as the queen. She's very strong but at the same time very young. Ewan McGregor is the perfect mix of a young Harrison Ford and a young Alec Guinness. He's extremely relaxed and strong. All the things that Alec Guinness is.

Giving his imagination free rein, Lucas' movie included some of his most outlandish imagery to date.

George Lucas: There are a lot more costumes, a lot more designs, and a lot more hairdos! If you don't like my hairdos in *Star Wars*, they will drive you nuts in this film. I like them.

Trisha Biggar (Costume Design): *The Phantom Menace* was a huge project. The opportunity to devise various planetary groups from top-to-toe was a wonderful challenge and such good fun. When you've got non-human bodies, it's quite difficult to create things for them to wear that will flatter and enhance their body shape without making the audience aware of the mechanics working underneath. George and I had long meetings where we looked at fabrics and mock-ups. There were also department meetings where he discussed historical or ethnic references he was interested in taking bits from and giving them a twist. He had clear ideas about how he saw various planetary groups. There were costumes that were completely new and some that link back to the original films such as the Tatooine outfits and the Jedi robes. The costumes for the

5 / The Jedi confront Darth Maul as the Sith emerge to menace the galaxy.

6 / Queen Amidala (Natalie Portman) flanked by her loyal handmaidens.

7 /

7 /

▶ Naboo were very interesting to do because we printed distinctive designs onto fabrics and used various dye techniques, which allowed us to incorporate modern fabrics with antique pieces.

The film was shot at Leavesden Studios, a former Rolls Royce factory. The large scale of the production created a challenge for David Tattersall, the director of photography, wherever filming took place.

David Tattersall (Director of Photography): Some of the sets at Leavesden were enormous. The main Theed Palace hangar was 275 feet long. One side of the set was completely blue screen and we had to light it evenly all the way down. We came up with a system of new lights that were designed and built called JAK FLOS. There were florescent units that were twice the power of anything that was available at the time. It gives us a much brighter, even quality of light than was ever possible. In the desert, the temperature was quite tricky

for us, technically. The film started to melt! So we had a careful routine of keeping the unexposed film in an airconditioned vehicle and the camera covered with cooling devices.

Perhaps Lucas' biggest gamble was with Jar Jar Binks, an amphibious Gungan who also happened to be a completely computer-generated character; making cinematic history as being the first of his kind.

George Lucas: Jar Jar Binks was a very hard character to figure out. He has hard dialogue to understand and make work; almost like Yoda times ten! Ahmed Best took to it. He really got it and turned that dialogue into a real language and turned Jar Jar into a real character.

Ahmed Best (Jar Jar Binks): A lot of my movement for Jar Jar came from breakdancing. My first audition for George Lucas was a motion-capture session. Robin Gurland, the casting director,

brought me into a room with all these infrared cameras and a number of people sitting behind computers. They gave me a skin-tight suit to put on, like a body glove, and six-inch wooden platform sneakers. I looked like an aerobics instructor from hell! I thought, *What am I doing here?* Before George arrived, I was asked to walk in the suit. I had developed this walk that was between a cool 50s bop and a glide across the floor, a bit like a moonwalk but moving forward. As I was doing this walk, George walks in. He was really cool about it, I'm sure he's seen weirder things in his time.

Best's skill at improvisation was called into action on set as he established Jar Jar's distinctive gait.

Ahmed Best: I pretty much had to imagine I was an amphibian creature. Nobody knows what this amphibian creature is going to move like or sound like, what will make him excited or sad. He's not human, so I came to him from a

7 / Qui-Gon and Obi-Wan use their knowledge of the Force and skill with lighsabers to escape a battle droid ambush.

8 / Jake Lloyd and Natalie Portman pose on location in Tunisia.

9 / Groundbreaking digital characters Jar Jar Binks (Ahmed Best) and Boss Nass (Brian Blessed) confer.

10 / Ray Park and Liam Neeson film the fight between Darth Maul and Qui-Gon.

left-field perspective. He can't be like a human being. There's a whole honesty in Jar Jar. He's not afraid to be who he is.

On set, I had a Jar Jar costume; I didn't have makeup on my face but I had Jar Jar's head on top of my head. It was hot and I didn't have a double so I had to stay out all day. Everyone else had doubles, but I didn't because nobody else could fit the suit! They made the suit especially for my body.

British actor Brian Blessed, best known for his often bombastic performances and larger than life personality played Boss Nass, the ruler of the Gungans.

Brian Blessed (Boss Nass):
I knew that Boss Nass was something quite unique and legendary. I seized the part with both hands. He is amazingly real. The expressions on my face come

though the computer. If you go in there and treat it like a robot, you are killing the scene. You have to interact with the actors. You have to affect them. The technology is an aid to becoming Boss Nass.

The only familiar human face from the original trilogy, Ian McDiarmid returned to play the not-yet Emperor as he plots his way to ultimate power by unseating the Supreme Chancellor, Valorum, played by veteran actor, Terence Stamp.

Ian McDiarmid (Palpatine):
[Returning to play the character as a younger man] was a rare experience, if not a unique one. I suppose I got to know Palpatine retrospectively. Like everybody else, I rushed to see the *Star Wars* Special Edition in 1997 but that was all I did really. I remembered him and what he feels quite

clearly. One just looks at contemporary politicians and then play the role as you would any straightforward naturalistic part. Of course, I—and a large number of the audience!—have in the back of my mind the fact that this is the most evil person who's ever dominated a planet, let alone the universe.

Terence Stamp (Valorum):
I asked George what Valorum was like and he said, "He's a good man but he's beleaguered —a bit like Bill Clinton."

I had good backup. I was working with the wondrous Natalie Portman, and I had a little scene with Ewan McGregor and Liam Neeson.

I had wonderful clothes! The wardrobe department had found wonderful fabric. I am aware of a shift into character when I start putting the costume on. ▶

 8 /

9 /

 10 /

12 /

The production headed back to Tunisia to film scenes that revealed that Luke Skywalker's homeworld was also his father's, as we meet Anakin Skywalker on Tatooine.

Hugh Quarshie (Captain Panaka): I was wearing a leather jerkin on top of a woollen coat with leather gloves and boots, and a big leather cap. When you are standing on a dune in 140-degree heat, all you are thinking is *Please don't make a mistake on this take!*

However, the production was blighted when a storm hit the set in Tunisia, causing damage to much-needed props.

Ewan McGregor (Obi-Wan Kenobi): Tunisia is so mind-blowingly huge, it kind of puts you in your place. When the storm hit the set, Rick McCallum was running around fixing the problem. He was in his element and we just carried on filming. George said, "Oh, this a is a good omen! This happened on the first one!" The crew pulled it all back together.

Hugh Quarshie: The desert is the last place on Earth that you would think there would be a hurricane and a thunderstorm. But there was one and it destroyed half the set. Yet George was unflustered by it. He just said, "These things happen." He's a cool guy.

Rick McCallum: Our crew did a remarkable job and not even Mother Nature slowed us down! The storm that hit the set was so fierce that planks of wood were blown through the metal walls of some of our equipment trucks. The crew just pulled it all together and fixed everything, keeping us on schedule.

The role of Queen Amidala, the future wife of Anakin Skywalker and mother of Luke and Leia was played by Natalie Portman.

Natalie Portman (Queen Amidala): The queen is fourteen years old but she has all this power. Yet she's also kind of naive. She's very smart, and compassionate, and cares about her people. She's not a selfish ruler. I've

never done a film where they would put a teenage girl in charge. In real life, they don't usually put girls in power.

Star Wars is very simple and very honest. It's kind of like George. He's certainly not simple—he's one of the most brilliant men I've ever met—but he is very direct and honest. He's not pretentious in the least. He never acts above anyone. He's never condescending. I think he's like the movie, because it has depth to it. It has a meaning and messages underneath. He really based it on mythology and fables, so it is a universal and timeless story. It's not trying to be fancy; it's allowing everyone to enjoy it on a different level.

Working on such a film with so many visual effects meant that the young actress had to accrue a new acting discipline as she learned to perform against blue-screen sets.

Natalie Portman: Working on blue screen is weird, because there's a lot more to concentrate on than just

11 / Jake Lloyd befriends a droid on set.

12 / Obi-Wan goes it alone as he battles Darth Maul.

13 /

acting and saying lines. You need to know where you are looking and where your eyeline is. Sometimes you'll be looking at a blue screen but you are supposed to be looking into someone's eyes, but your eyes focus differently when you are looking at a wall or if you are looking at a dot. But they can't put a dot on the blue screen, so you have everyone focussing on the same point and staying out of the way of a certain character if a certain character is there, but they are not really there. It was the first time I ever felt like acting was a job. The finished result looks so awesome. I can brag about how it looks because it has nothing to do with me! It was weird to watch myself walk around a place I've never been to.

Hugh Quarshie: Natalie Portman is a great actress. She has a lot to do and think about in Episode I. I don't think I was that focused

at her age. In *Star Wars,* you've just got your imagination and the assurance of the director. It's a style of performance that has to be learned. I think it's as valid a skill as knowing how to read five lines of iambic pentameter.

Another key aspect of the film was the combat. Lucas was keen that audiences see Jedi in their prime take on their foes, including a dangerous Sith Lord, the instantly iconic Darth Maul.

Nick Gillard (Stunt Coordinator): I figured that if a Jedi had chosen a sword, they'd have to be really good with it. So I took the essence of all the great sword techniques from kendo through to saber, épée, and foil, and tried to flow them all together. I couldn't have wanted more from Liam Neeson and Ewan McGregor. Sometimes they learned moves ten minutes before we shot a scene. They were that good.

Ewan McGregor: My cloak was so huge. I was always falling over in it. When I was fighting in it, my lightsaber was always going up my sleeve or under my cloak. It's a good idea on paper but was pretty hard to wear!

Ray Park (Darth Maul): I went to help Nick Gillard rehearse a fight to show George Lucas. He said it might help me, because they were looking for somebody who could do action to play Darth Maul. We rehearsed for a week and then on the Friday we filmed it and showed George Lucas. From there, I had a call from Rick McCallum telling me I had the job.

I could spin the double-bladed lightsaber around and give them moves they didn't expect. I could be more creative. We worked from morning to late evening, working on different stunts and acrobatic moves, just getting them 100-percent right.

13 / Liam Neeson's stunt double, Rob Inch, looks on as Ray Park flips into action as Darth Maul.

14 / Ray Park, making his movie debut as Darth Maul, one of the most enduring icons of the movie.

"
To be part of a legend, to be part of a modern myth and to play the young Alec Guinness was an honor.
"

Ewan McGregor

▶ The last fight Ewan McGregor and I did was really fiery. We really went for it. He fed off me and I fed off him. The energy we had was really good.

Despite the fierce confidence of the character, Ray Park, in his first acting role, took a while to feel at ease. Thankfully, the makeup department helped him to get into character.

Ray Park: At first I wasn't sure how the character was supposed to be played, but George seemed so cool about everything and he made me feel more confident. People on the set would get scared when I had the lenses in my eyes and the teeth and makeup. They couldn't look me in the eye when I was speaking to them.

One very popular returning character was Yoda, as played by returning performer Frank Oz.

Frank Oz (Yoda): Yoda is very hard work. It's really five days of rehearsal for two days of shooting, because every single move, and every blink has to be worked out. However, it is so nice to see an old friend like Yoda and to dig a little deeper into the character, because it's more acting than performing. The Muppets are characters I perform with, but with Yoda I act more in the sense that I trust the

script and the character more, and I'm not thinking about pleasing the audience. I did two weeks on *The Empire Strikes Back*, and *Return of the Jedi* was two days.

One lucky fan managed to secure a key role in the film, proving popular enough to return for both of the next two Episodes.

Samuel L. Jackson (Mace Windu): People always ask you the question, "Are there any directors that you haven't worked with that you want to work with?" I was on a chat show in the U.K. and said "George Lucas." When I was shooting a movie in Vallejo, I got a call inviting me to the Skywalker Ranch to meet George as he had heard I was interested in the movies. Just an opportunity to go to the Ranch was cool with me.

Although his time on the set was brief, the veteran actor enjoyed every moment.

Samuel L. Jackson: I was awed. It's pretty awesome to just show up on the set. It's something that I'd always imagined, and all of a sudden I was in it! I was only there for four days and George only gave me the six pages I was in on the days we were filming. The *Star Wars* set actually had more of a low-budget feel to it. There were none of the huge-star

trappings. There were no huge trailers. There were no P.A.s running around with their heads cut off. There was a calmness on set. It was totally laidback.

I actually met actors I wouldn't know if they walked into my house today, because they were covered in makeup. There was one guy I affectionally referred to as "calamari" and there was another guy that looked like a giant Lhasa Apso and there was a guy with a duck on his head!

Working with Yoda is like working with a great actor. He was there, totally involved, with great facial expressions, and great line-reading. He was totally cool. Yoda is there, not Frank Oz. You hear action and Frank gets in there and Yoda sits up and comes to life. Then George says "cut" and Frank lets go of Yoda and he slumps over. The guys are still operating his ears and eyes so he looks like he's not feeling well! It's like, "Somebody help Yoda!"

Jackson wasn't the only actor who took delight in appearing in the movie. Ewan McGregor was pleased to be chosen to play the young Obi-Wan Kenobi, a role first essayed by Alec Guinness.

Ewan McGregor: To be part of a legend, to be part of a modern myth and to play the young Alec Guinness was an incredible honor. ▶

15 / The stoic Mace Windu, as played by Samuel L. Jackson.

I was six when the first movie came out, so as soon as I heard there was a possibility of playing this part, it became a mission because of what these films meant to me as a kid. They were like fairy-tale movies and were completely engrossing. I used to play *Star Wars* all the time and now I'm being paid to do it.

I worked hard on getting the voice right. I did a lot of work with a dialogue coach to try and get a younger-sounding version of Sir Alec Guinness' voice. It's quite a trick to imagine what his younger voice sounded like because in a lot of his early films, he's using an accent. I studied him in the first *Star Wars* film. I'm always watching the scene in his house where he gives Luke the lightsaber. He's got such a specific voice that we associate with an older man, a kind of fatherly voice. There's something paternal about him and calming. He knows what he's about.

In every area in the studio, there seemed to be 300 people working away. It was incredible to see the props. I was screaming out loud when I saw them, but the guys working in the prop room looked at me as if they understood, so it was

all right! It was quite a moment; meeting R2-D2 for the first time. It's a bit like meeting the queen. He was just wheeled out casually. I love owning my lightsaber. I can't have it in my hand and not give it a few twirls. Every day had a *Star Wars* moment or two where I thought, *My God—I'm in Star Wars!*

Although not quite a Sith Lord yet, Anakin, as played by nine-year-old Jake Lloyd was not new to *Star Wars*, showing where his allegiances lay at an early age.

Jake Lloyd (Anakin Skywalker): When I was six, I was Darth Vader for Halloween. Now I got to be a Jedi again! Anakin is a lot like me. I love doing mechanics, and he is one mechanical kid! I waited for two years to get the part. I auditioned twice.

Ewan McGregor: I never worked with a child actor as good as Jake Lloyd. He is phenomenal. I found myself saying, "How many takes are we going to do of this scene?" and then I'd look at him and feel ashamed because he didn't complain at all.

16 / The second unit crew get some shots of the alien senators.

17 / Senator Palpatine takes his seat on the senate with Queen Amidala.

18 / A stripped-down C-3PO voiced by Anthony Daniels.

Pernilla August took on the role of Anakin's mother, Shmi.

Pernilla August (Shmi Skywalker): George Lucas told me Shmi had come from another galaxy, a Swedish one, so she was allowed to have an accent.

Returning to the role of C-3PO, actor Anthony Daniels was surprised by a certain twist in George Lucas' story.

Anthony Daniels: George explained that Threepio was built by Anakin. I was shocked and horrified! The last person whose hand you would expect Threepio to come from would be Darth Vader's! I think See-Threepio's awkwardness is down to him. I don't know where else it comes from. Could you put the whole of his predicament down to his being built by a nine-year-old who wants to go podracing?

The music, as for the previous films, was provided by the incomparable John Williams.

John Williams (Composer): *The Phantom Menace* has 120 minutes

17 /

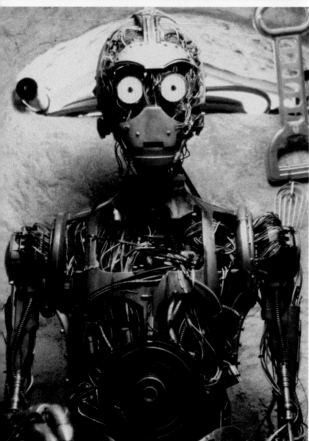

18 /

of very dense and active music, because it is all on an operatic scale. George always says that *Star Wars* is like a silent movie and it really is: the music underscores the emotion, but also the action, the starships, and the lightsaber fights. When you confront the need to create that volume of music in the weeks you have to do it, it's a daunting and challenging task, just getting the notes on paper. Then the challenge extends to creating material that is fresh and new, and that also has a connection and relationship to the old material in texture and thematic styles. Anakin has his theme, and if you listen carefully, you'll hear hints of what's to come in later incarnations.

Perhaps the best-loved piece of music Williams created for the film was the epic "Duel of the Fates."

John Williams: I was watching the duel between Darth Maul and Qui-Gon and it occurred to me that it might be wonderful to have voices as part of the music. I wanted to find a text that would offer vowel sounds, which is really the so-called noise that a chorus will make. We can't ever fully understand when a chorus sings the words, and in a dramatic sense, it's not important that we know the words, just that a chorus has a certain kind of sound.

I found an ancient Celtic text called "The Battle of the Trees." There is a stanza, which in English is; "Under the tongue root a fight most dread, while another rages behind in the head." The symbolism on the poetry is that the trees become animated and they become the warriors in the battle. At the end of the battle, the druid priest freezes them back into tree form. It gave an almost religious feeling to that duel as though they were fighting in a church. I had a translator put the text into a couple of languages. Celtic didn't have the vowels we needed. Greek and Latin were not remote enough. So I had it put into Sanskrit and we used the Sanskrit text just as syllables to intone the words "Dreaded fight that's here

or lingering the head." The piece really describes an unstoppable force of destiny, like the Force that George talks about.

The release of the movie in May 1999 won a new generation of fans of *Star Wars*, and renewed interest in the saga for many who were there the first time around.

Samuel L. Jackson: George has taken us to a place where you look around and see green people, blue people, hairy people, bald people, short people, tall people, skinny people, winged people, and nobody ever talks about what people look like. Everybody's just dealing with each other like there are no differences.

Ian McDiarmid: I was lucky enough to be involved in the first day of shooting, and the last. The first shot was quite an emotional moment. There was a degree of anticipation and tension on the set. We were all nervous. I wasn't in the last shot, but it involved an explosion. George with typical showman's instinct, waited, did the shot from various angles and various ways, and waited for the final moment to press bang.

Ahmed Best: The first time I saw the movie, I was sitting next to Harrison Ford. It was crazy looking at him, then looking at the movie, then looking at him to see his reaction. He was on the edge of his seat!

Rick McCallum: We had up to 1,800 people at one time working on the movie. We shot in four different countries. We designed and built everything. It was intense. The budget was $120 million and we came in at $115 million.

George Lucas: I got the film I set out to make this time. I was able to let my imagination run wild. I could dream up whatever I wanted to see, and, for the most part, I was able to pull it off. ☻

EVERY SAGA HAS A BEGINNING

STAR WARS
EPISODE I
THE PHANTOM MENACE™

STAR WARS   EPISODE I   THE PHANTOM MENACE
Starring LIAM NEESON   EWAN McGREGOR   NATALIE PORTMAN   JAKE LLOYD   IAN McDIARMID
Co-starring ANTHONY DANIELS   KENNY BAKER   PERNILLA AUGUST   FRANK OZ
Music by JOHN WILLIAMS   Produced by RICK McCALLUM

Written and Directed by
GEORGE LUCAS

Special Visual Effects and Animation by INDUSTRIAL LIGHT & MAGIC
A LUCASFILM LTD Production – A TWENTIETH CENTURY FOX Release
Soundtrack Available on SONY CLASSICAL Read the Novel from DEL REY BOOKS

W W W . S T A R W A R S . C O M

STAR WARS: THE PHANTOM MENACE

ESSENTIAL TRIVIA

The Phantom Menace is the first and only time we see the Jedi use their "Force run" ability in a *Star Wars* movie.

We're accustomed to seeing lightsabers used in combat, but for the first time, we see a lightsaber used to cut through a door!

Kitster, Ric Olié, Valorum, Fode and Beed, Sebulba, Sabé, Captain Tarpals, and Captain Panaka only appear in this movie.

Look out for *Pirates of the Carribean* star Keira Knightly as Padmé's loyal handmaiden, Sabé. Director Sofia Coppola plays another of Padmé's handmaidens, Saché.

Dominic West, star of *The Wire* (2002–2008), plays a Naboo guard.

The Phantom Menace marks the only time we see the "ripple effect" viewscreen on the Trade Federation ship in live-action. The sound effect was borrowed from an old *Flash Gordon* chapter serial.

The Phantom Menace is the only time we see Obi-Wan Kenobi without a beard in live-action.

Look out for the only shots in the movie in which Jar Jar isn't computer generated. For example, some occur in the scene where the hapless Gungan gets numbed by the podracer's power coupling.

Ewan McGregor is the nephew of Denis Lawson who played Wedge.

The queen's ship is a J-type 327 Nubian. The number 327 was also the number of the landing platform that the *Millennium Falcon* landed on in Cloud City in *The Empire Strikes Back*.

Visual effects supervisor John Knoll and his team had to write a computer program that had the sole purpose of governing the movements of the little cord hanging from Watto's belt.

George Lucas considered duality to be one of the main themes of the film, as seen in Padmé's double role as the queen and handmaiden, and Palpatine's duality. Other examples include the master/appentice relationships between Obi-Wan and Qui-Gon and between Darth Sidious and Darth Maul. There is also the symbiotic link between the Gungans and the Naboo.

The sound of the crowds at the podrace is a recording of a San Francisco 49ers' football game.

The name "Mace Windu" first appeared in George Lucas' original *Star Wars* story outlines, which began: "This is the story of Mace Windu, a revered Jedi-bendu of Opuchi."

The battle droid that Jar Jar Binks pushes over has a stylized "1138" on its back, a reference to George Lucas' *THX 1138*.

The triumphant parade music at the close of the film is actually a reworking of the Emperor's theme from *Return of the Jedi*.

Coruscant was first conceived by Ralph McQuarrie during development of the original trilogy. It was named years later by Timothy Zahn. Design director Doug Chiang adapted McQuarrie's designs for the new film, with a preview of the city appearing in the *Return of the Jedi* Special Edition.

George Lucas frequently used the term "lazer sword" in his early drafts of the story. Uniquely, Anakin uses the term in this film.

Watto's junkyard contains a Discovery spacepod from Stanley Kubrick's *2001: A Space Odyssey*.

Producer Rick McCallum and sound designer Ben Burtt have cameo roles as Naboo officials during the scene in which Palpatine arrives on Naboo.

The first scene shot for the film was Darth Maul's meeting with Darth Sidious on Coruscant. It was filmed on June 26, 1997.

Natalie Portman used her own voice for Padmé and played Queen Amidala with the kind of British accent that people did back in the days of old-school Hollywood.

Animation director Rob Coleman was concerned that Watto's trunk would prevent convincing speech animation, but design director Doug Chiang didn't want to alter his look. A compromise was reached by breaking one of his tusks and having him talk out of the corner of his mouth.

For the second episode of the *Star Wars* saga, George Lucas concocted a story of romance, played out against the backdrop of the outbreak of an intergalactic war. Acclaimed playwright Jonathan Hales, who had worked on Lucasfilm's *The Young Indiana Jones Chronicles* (1992-1993), served as co-writer on the script.

George Lucas (Writer/Director): *The Phantom Menace* was just for fun. A lot of things planted there start to pay off in *Attack of the Clones*. You begin to see the root of the problem, and it all starts, and in the next film, everything happens! I'm basically doing a three-act play over a period of ten years. The middle act is the hardest to deal with because you're adding more substance to the story—the plot thickens. This was a big concern for me in *The Empire Strikes Back* because it was the second movie. It had a lot at stake but it didn't have a beginning, middle, or end! I know now that whether it is an upper or a downer, it doesn't matter, as long as the story is told well. There are a lot of reverberations, scenes that are reprised between *Empire* and this film.

Jonathan Hales (Co-writer): You know before you start how the story is going to end, and that's part of the problem and part of the satisfaction of solving the problem. Episode II is not the story of a villain, it's about someone who is incredibly gifted but is trapped and almost doomed by his good qualities. The central idea, that Anakin is the Chosen One but is slowly turned to the dark side, has parallels to the story of Lucifer —the bright angel who falls.

George Lucas: The fact that this movie is character-driven does not necessarily mean that I delve that much deeper into the characters, because, stylistically, it's not a

3 /

character study, it's an action-adventure film and I have to stay true to that concept.

The movie made history as the first major film to be shot entirely on digital film.

Anthony Daniels (C-3PO): At the time of the first *Star Wars* film, I'd never been in a movie, so I was amazed that the only person who saw the movie was the guy with the camera piece to his eye. Now, with permission, one stands behind George, looking at a three-foot plasma screen watching the take.

George Lucas: With these kinds of movies, you have to shoot 100 percent of a live-action movie and then you have to shoot 100 percent of an animated movie. You have to film it twice.

The film featured a myriad of fascinating characters for the writers to work with, including some old favorites.

Jonathan Hales: Anakin and Obi-Wan are fun. Though they are master and apprentice, they do have a spirited and humorous relationship. Yoda is tricky to write for. George is great at writing Yoda. He's also really good at writing for Threepio and the droids. He's graduated in those characters.

Joining the illustrious company of Jake Lloyd and Sebastian Shaw, Hayden Christensen made his *Star Wars* debut as Anakin Skywalker.

Hayden Christensen (Anakin Skywalker): It was tough [to keep my casting secret]. I didn't even tell my friends—just my best

1 / George Lucas directs Anthony Daniels as C-3PO at a very familar location. (Previous spread)

2 / The droids reunited in an image evocative of *A New Hope*.

3 / The Neimoidian's expressive facial features were operated via remote control.

4 / Hayden Christensen as Anakin Skywalker.

friend and family knew. I just walked around with a huge grin on my face. I had a meeting with Robin Gurland, the casting director, and talked about my experiences with acting and what I was doing. She put that on videotape and showed that to George. Then, two months later I met with George at Skywalker Ranch. We just sat down and talked—not about *Star Wars*. We didn't even talk about the film industry, it was just chitchat. I went back two months later to do a screen test with Natalie Portman. We read a scene that was not in the final film. I was content with that experience. They gave me an Episode I cap and a mug, so I was happy!

Ultimately cast in the part, Christensen played opposite Natalie Portman, returning as the former Queen of Naboo.

Hayden Christensen: I wanted to be a part of every aspect that I could and be involved in every way possible. Everyone working on *Star Wars* is the best at what they do. I had never worked with blue screen before but it wasn't dissimilar from doing theater, because it demands more of your imagination. You have to be able to visualize everything around you.

The actor found the challenges of the complex role fulfilling.

Hayden Christensen: The most fulfilling part of playing Anakin is being given material in which you're able to make such a drastic and archetypal transition from good to evil. What George impressed on me most was to be as subtle as possible. Subtlety reads so much, especially when you are trying to define such an intricate balance. We were very specific when we wanted to show the dark side of Anakin.

I was excited by what George Lucas expected from me as an actor in terms of showing emotional range.

I tried to steal some of Vader's physicality, like his posture as well as the monotone demeanor he has.

Even though *Star Wars* movies have a gripping emotional quality to them, people weren't going in every day and crying and leaving emotionally exhausted. I feel like I got the chance to do that.

One scene in particular proved pivotal for the character.

Hayden Christensen: The garage scene at the Lars homestead was particularly important to me. Up until that point, Anakin has

5 / Anakin and Padmé embark on a highly dangerous romance.

6 / Padmé marries Anakin at the climax of the film.

7 / Disguised, the Jedi and the senator go into hiding.

that childish, dismissive tone. He has the arrogance that a child has. So it was important to me when he is at the emotional and mental brink that he breaks down and cries and displays his emotions in the way a child would. I put a lot of effort into that scene.

Natalie Portman (Padmé): It starts out that Padmé's relationship with Anakin is one of mentor. She's known him only as a little boy prior to this episode, so when they re-encounter each other, she still treats him like a little kid. George worked with me to make me seem older than

Anakin, to make it believable that she would boss him around and look at him as a little boy—at least for the first half of the film, until it becomes more of a romance.

As romantic as the finished scene was, Portman and Christensen found the dinner scene, complete with levitating fruit, amusing to film.

Natalie Portman: We felt pretty stupid biting into fruit that didn't exist. But, still, it was a fun scene to shoot. I don't think George was entirely satisfied with the dialogue

he had written for the scene, because he told us to improvise—and of course it got inappropriate very quickly!

For Portman, freeing Amidala of her royal duties was an important step for the character.

Natalie Portman: Amidala resigned as queen because she believes that is the way a rightful government is conducted; that one leader should not be in power for too long. The fact that Amidala doesn't start a relationship with Anakin when she has feelings for him shows she doesn't really think ▶

of her own desires before her role as leader of the people. She's an idealistic person. She's a good and honest person and, because of that, sometimes she's a naïve person. She doesn't imagine that other people aren't as good as she is. She's strong and intelligent, but her weakness is she doesn't think about what she needs for herself. She is always thinking about her career and role as a leader as opposed to her role as a woman and a human being. She's much happier in the role of leader.

It comes into play how strong and smart a character Carrie Fisher portrayed because I think a lot of that is passed from parent to child. I think George wrote Amidala as a strong, smart character but it helped to know that I had this [actress] before me who portrayed her as a fiery woman. I met Carrie at an event and she introduced me as her mother!

Making his Star Wars debut was screen veteran Christopher Lee, who provided a chilling performance as sophisticated Jedi turned Sith Lord, Count Dooku, who was paired with returning villain, Palpatine, played, once again, by Ian McDiarmid.

Rick McCallum (Producer): Christopher Lee is someone who George has always liked. He always wanted to work with him and thought that this was the chance.

George Lucas: I didn't want to keep creating bigger monsters. I decided to make Dooku an elegant old gentleman. After Darth Sidious loses his first apprentice, he has to come up with a new apprentice and decides he needs somebody who is already trained. The point is that he has turned one Jedi, so he could turn another Jedi.

Christopher Lee (Count Dooku): George Lucas told me the film would be a lot of fun and that's a word that should be in capital

letters! In order to have fun on a film, you should be able to relax, and that comes from the top.

Ian McDiarmid (Palpatine): Palpatine is a man of mystery. That is how he exercises and maintains and increases his power—by choosing what he is public about. He's the greatest political manipulator of all time. Probably the most interesting aspect of the part for me is that he appears to be a hard-working politician but underneath that he is an evil soul. The undercurrents are always there in his mind and his gut. Everything he does is an act of pure hypocrisy, and that's interesting to play. Palpatine is a supreme actor. He's very charming, extra professional; and for those

9 /

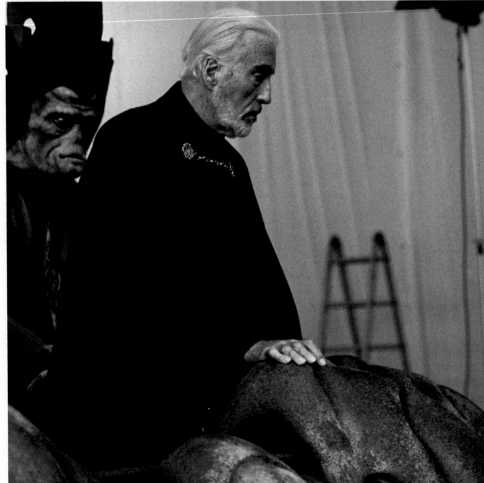

10 /

looking for clues, that's almost where you can see them.

There is a scene in *Attack of the Clones* where tears almost appear in his eyes. These are crocodile tears; he can just turn them on. The pure exercise of power is what he is all about. That's the only thing he's interested in. He is more evil than the devil; at least Satan fell.

Christopher Lee: On my first morning on the set, I filmed the scene where Count Dooku is escaping from the battle on his bike. Francis Ford Coppola was on the set, sitting next to George, watching me while I was shooting the scene against blue screen with the wind machine blowing my cloak around behind me. We shot the scene for quite a long time, three or four minutes. Francis came up to me and said, "Christopher, that was all there: the whole character, the whole story. I could read the entire situation on your face." At this stage, I didn't know if he was joking and said, "Thank you very much, but I don't think I changed my expression once!" I thought it was very funny.

Lee's close friendship with the actor behind another *Star Wars* villain, Peter Cushing, was

instrumental in his agreeing to appear in the film.

Christopher Lee: Peter Cushing meant a great deal in my life. We were very close friends. He was an important reason I was happy to take the role in *Attack of the Clones* because I was following him. I wrote Peter a letter when the first film was released saying, "What on Earth is a Grand Moff?" He wrote back to say he had no idea!

I didn't ask George Lucas the dreaded question, "What's my motivation?" but I was intrigued by Dooku and asked George to tell me about the Sith. Filming was held up by fifteen minutes while he told me their history.

George Lucas took a hands-on approach to the making of the film, even getting involved in sculpting a bust of Count Dooku.

Peter Walpole (Set decorator): George Lucas had a specific idea as to how he wanted the Count Dooku bust done. He wanted it in the style of Auguste Rodin. The sculptors couldn't quite grasp what George wanted. Eventually, George actually got his hands into the clay and started making it himself! ▶

8 / George Lucas directs an amused Natalie Portman as they film the dinner scene.

9 / Christopher Lee and George Lucas work on the Geonosian arena sequence.

10 / Portman and Hayden Christensen share a joke as a performer in a blue outfit—to be replaced with a Geonosian warrior—drives them along.

11 / Obi-Wan (Ewan McGregor) takes flight.

12 / Obi-Wan's investigation into the strange goings on on Kamino leads to an encounter with Boba and Jango Fett.

13 / Ewan McGregor and Hayden Christensen share a joke on set.

▶ Reprising his role as Obi-Wan Kenobi, Ewan McGregor welcomed George Lucas' nods to the other films in the saga.

Ewan McGregor (Obi-Wan Kenobi): I got to go on a detective spree and it was really good! I cut a bounty hunter's arm off, which is cool because Obi-Wan cuts an arm off in *A New Hope*! He's obviously a bit of an arm cutter isn't he? There are moments in Jango Fett's apartment when it's like the scene on the Death Star when he is going around with his hood.

With an older Anakin Skywalker to play off, the chance came to establish the two Jedi's relationship as referenced in the original film.

Ewan McGregor: Obi-Wan and Anakin are like two old friends who have been together a long time and spent too much time together. They argue, but as friends do. Obi-Wan is worried that Anakin is too headstrong and overconfident, and Anakin thinks the reverse of Obi-Wan—that he is staid, boring, and does everything by the book. They've been together every day

since Qui-Gon died, I think. You can start to put the pieces together of how Anakin gets to be Darth Vader. You can see it in Hayden's performance; you can imagine Anakin going to the dark side because of his frustrations, his ego, and his pain.

Hayden Christensen: Anakin feels that he's being oppressed and not being given his freedom to go and explore and be the Jedi he wants to be. Obi-Wan wants to go by the book and he doesn't want Anakin to rush through his training. It's

almost like a *Butch Cassidy and the Sundance Kid* (1969) type of relationship. It's a little eerie when you remember what happens later, but you just forget about that and let the struggles and obstacles he has to overcome manifest themselves and let that guide you.

Samuel L. Jackson (Mace Windu): Mace Windu has known Obi-Wan Kenobi for a very long time. Mace was a contemporary of Qui-Gon Jinn. He understood his faults and admired his qualities and can see that Obi-Wan has taken on some of Qui-Gon's strong-headedness by wanting to train Anakin Skywalker.

Ewan McGregor found the experience of working with blue screen challenging but was quick to praise the final result.

Ewan McGregor: Working with blue screen can be frustrating a lot of the time because there is nothing there, which for an actor is not great. There's no interaction. It becomes technical. There's nothing to play off. There is something rewarding about cracking a scene with other actors. With blue screen, you perform a scene and it feels like nothing has happened!

There was a speeder chase, which we filmed on a speeder that was rocking about and it actually

made me feel sick! It was like going on a fairground ride over and over again. The actual sequence was something to behold but it's like watching somebody else because the bit you filmed was surrounded by blue. You see the world around you in the final edit.

The frustrations of not knowing what's around you don't show in the film. All the characters in *Star Wars* are space traveling and the fact that there are thousands of speeders going past us outside the windows is an everyday occurrence. It creates more of a sense of belief that they are in this world.

Christopher Lee: Good grief, [the interrogation scene] was difficult to film. Poor Ewan was spinning around, strung up by his jockstrap and turning the air blue. I don't think he was comfortable. ▶

12 /

14 /

▶ After appearing as a puppet in *The Phantom Menace*, it was time for a certain Jedi Master to go digital.

Frank Oz (Yoda): I thought George should [make Yoda digital]. As long as the character is true and pure. That's the most important thing. As long as it doesn't look like an effect, it's a case of whatever works for the audience.

George Lucas: We were trying not to make Yoda look realistic. We were trying to make him look like a puppet. We didn't want him to be a different character. They built a puppet for *The Phantom Menace* with a different kind of material and it gave him a slightly different nature. He was younger so we rationalized that we could get away with that. For *Attack of the Clones*, we were in the middle ground between the Yoda of *The Phantom Menace* and Yoda as we know him in *The Empire Strikes Back*.

Samuel L. Jackson: Everyone is in a secondary position to Yoda. We aren't as intuitive or as strong, mentally or spiritually. Yoda is incorruptible, and unfathomable in a lot of ways.

Christopher Lee: The fight between Dooku and Yoda had a number of variations. We started it in Australia and finished in London. It was quite a long process. There was some concern about Yoda jumping on my back as it was written in the script. I remember saying, "We're in danger of an unintentional laugh here."

Samuel L. Jackson's Mace Windu returned, taking a more active role, as he brandished his unique purple-bladed lightsaber in stunning combat sequences.

Samuel L. Jackson: I've watched swashbuckling films all my life. I was a huge Errol Flynn fan when I was a kid and this is the next step in the fencing age. It would have been a shame to participate in a film like this and never get to use

15 /

my lightsaber! Nick Gillard put together a very exciting and incredible fight for me; and since I was supposedly the second-baddest person in the universe, I dispensed people pretty quickly, using as little energy as possible.

Mace is a voice of reason. He thinks before he speaks. He's pretty calculating, mostly even-tempered, and he's not to be trifled with. He knows that the war is coming and he has a pretty good idea who is behind it.

14 / Samuel L. Jackson and George Lucas discuss a scene.

15 / The Jedi are surrounded as Dooku gains the upper hand.

16 / Yoda makes his digital debut!

The movie's many emerging characters include Jango, father to a fan-favorite character, Boba Fett.

George Lucas: Boba Fett is a background character, but I needed a device, a bounty hunter to do things. That particular bounty hunter had become a rather popular character and even though people were writing all kinds of things about where he came from, in my mind he was always connected to the stormtroopers. I realized that

I could use Jango Fett as the bounty hunter and he would be Boba's father and then it all fell into place. But even if he wasn't a popular character, it would probably have fallen into place. There are lots of little stories in this film, sidebars of how things came to be. Some of it was part of the original backstory, mainly the main characters, but all the secondary characters were added later.

Temuera Morrison (Jango Fett): When Robin Gurland called to tell me I had the part, she said, "You're playing Jango Fett, Boba Fett's father," and I just said "Great, that's good!" and hung up. Then I said, "Who the hell is that?" I'm the original bounty hunter. Whatever Boba Fett is, he takes from me.

Like many actors, Morrison found that putting on his costume was key to finding his character.

Temuera Morrison: As soon as I had the costume on, I started jumping around the costume department. I cleared an area and was running around, doing some of the fight moves. I couldn't help it—I got quite excited. You get most of your stuff from the outfit because it gives you that texture. You get all these organic feelings when you're in costume. You have to walk in it, which gives you a little bit of character as well. I knew I only had the opportunity here and there—when the helmet comes off—to shine. I tried to make the most of those moments to try and get a nice flow. When the helmet was on my head, I had trouble breathing and seeing, so there were a lot of curse words coming from beneath my helmet! The team tried to make me as comfortable as they could but when the rain was coming down, it's not that easy! I had a lot of fight sequences in the rain and I was initially quite willing to do it. But after a day or two, I let the stunt guy have his turn.

17 / Temuera Morrison and Daniel Logan as Jango and Boba Fett in the *Slave I* cockpit.

18 / Morrison suits up as Jango prepares to kill some Jedi.

19 / Morrison and Logan as the Fetts.

18 /

▶ Morrison's first scene was the confrontation between Jango and Obi-Wan Kenobi.

Temuera Morrison: I was very nervous when I started on the movie. I had to resort to my Maori Warrior side in order to increase my confidence in playing such a strong character with so much backstory. I played some of those initial scenes as if I was in a poker game and I had an ace up my sleeve. I tried not to let Ewan McGregor's splendid performance intimidate me whatsoever. I was so nervous at times, but George Lucas would say, "Just pretend it's another day in the Olive Grove."

Jango has a strong bond with his son, Boba, which reflected Morrison's relationship with the actor playing him, Daniel Logan.

Temuera Morrison: I took Daniel under my arm and treated him like my own son.

Daniel Logan (Boba Fett): *Attack of the Clones* felt like a second home and family to me. One of my fondest memories is racing with Ewan McGregor on the golf carts around the lot. We got into some trouble, but it was fun!

Ewan McGregor: When Daniel opened the door and saw me as Obi-Wan, George wanted him to look suspicious of me. I just told

him to pretend that I had done a really bad fart. Surprise and bad smells register a similar expression in the face. He was brilliant!

One of the saga's longest-tenured actors, Anthony Daniels was sad to see a touching scene between C-3PO and Padmé was excised from the final cut of the film.

Anthony Daniels: In *Attack of the Clones*, I wanted to be more connected to the character and do the puppetry myself. I really toned up my muscles to carry this heavy thing around on my shoulders, head, and knees. We shot the whole thing as the puppet, including the scene where Padmé walked in and Threepio was feeling a bit sad and

explained that it was difficult being this way. She says, "Ahh, that's not a problem" and finds some bits and dresses him up. Unfortunately, we had to lose that because there wasn't time in the storyline. George thought it was too soft and romantic.

We had a special rig with me in it where she approached with a chest piece, and then we came back as she was putting the face on. I was wearing bits stuck on with fridge magnets so she could stick the face on. Threepio was just ecstatic. For the first time, he was complete. And all that got cut out. I had to go back and do everything as the rust bucket, which is actually the gold suit painted rusty on green screen, so I had to remember everything

Joel Edgerton: Most people talk about Uncle Owen as this awful character because he's trying to stop Luke from fulfilling his dreams. But I always saw him as a father figure acting in Luke's best interests. I wanted to play him as a nice and somewhat eager country boy. He was probably cautious about the outside world and eager to understand and be told stories about places. There's a certain naivety about him. I'm sure he was a bit of a Luke himself, working away and wondering whether or not to go and explore.

Ending on a dramatic cliffhanger, *Attack of the Clones* set the stage for the final chapter in the prequel trilogy.

Jonathan Hales: The bleak turn the story takes creates a tougher quandary because, unlike *The Empire Strikes Back*, which was leading into the triumphant *Return of the Jedi*, *Attack of the Clones* is followed by the darkest film of the trilogy. Episode II ends on a mixture of triumph and tragedy.

Samuel L. Jackson: *Attack of the Clones* is a high-tech film and George has always been known as an innovator. He's doing something new and different in a new format. We were stepping into the next generation of moviemaking. You think of George having all of this technical acumen, but I remember going to his house to watch the trailer for the first time. We were in a screening room, and he couldn't get the screening room to work. His son, Jett, had to come and fix it and all of a sudden it was working! ☻

23 /

I'd done. I was very sorry that sequence got left out because you saw the backstory of Threepio, and it explained why he might be a bit nervous.

Meanwhile, his counterpart R2-D2 showed no sign of nerves on set.

Ewan McGregor: R2-D2 standing still and twirling his head and whistling is perfect. But when we started to move him around, that's when the fun starts! He falls over a lot or gets stuck on gratings.

The film also introduced the younger versions of Owen and Beru, before they take responsibility for the young Luke Skywalker.

Joel Edgerton (Owen Lars): We got some pages from the original *Star Wars* of the scene where Owen and Luke are talking. I read Owen's lines and Robin Gurland, the casting director, read as Luke. Then I asked her if we could switch characters. It seemed a more appropriate way to get into a young man's headspace, so I felt more like a young man talking to an authority figure.

Bonnie Piesse (Beru Whitesun): Robin Gurland had me read the original Beru's lines during my audition. Leading up to that, I spent a lot of time watching Shelagh Fraser's performance and getting a sense for how she held herself, and how she spoke. I wanted to show the younger, more innocent side of Beru.

24 /

STAR WARS

EPISODE II

ATTACK OF THE CLONES

STAR WARS: ATTACK OF THE CLONES

ESSENTIAL TRIVIA

As Jango Fett enters *Slave I* on Kamino following his fight against Obi-Wan Kenobi, he knocks his head on the door frame. This is a reference to the infamous stormtrooper who does the same thing in *A New Hope*.

Just before Anakin leaves the Lars homestead to find his mother, he casts a shadow eerily similar to that of Darth Vader. This was not a deliberate visual effect, but just a coincidence.

Running at 140 minutes, this is the longest of the prequels and, until *The Last Jedi*, was the longest of the *Star Wars* films.

Anthony Daniels (C-3PO) and Ahmed Best (Jar Jar Binks) both cameo as patrons of the bar in which the Jedi pursue Zam Wesell.

The Twi'lek Jedi Aayla Secura first appeared in a comic book series called *Star Wars: Republic*. George Lucas liked the look of the character so he included her in the film.

No physical clone armor was made for the film. All the clones were rendered using CGI.

According to the visual effects supervisor, John Knoll, a shaak, one of the big cow-like creatures from the fields of Naboo, appears as an asteroid in the chase scene between Jango and Obi-Wan.

A deleted scene revealed that the bust Obi-Wan was looking at in the Jedi Archive was of Count Dooku.

The yellow speeder that Anakin and Obi-Wan use to chase Zam Wesell was inspired by the yellow '32 Ford coupe from George Lucas' *American Graffiti* (1973).

The large aiwha whale seen flying out of the waves on Kamino was originally illustrated by Ralph McQuarrie for the Cloud City scenes in *The Empire Strikes Back*.

The original script for the movie bore the tongue-in-cheek title, "Jar Jar's Big Adventure."

According to his backstory, Dooku is a Count of Serenno.

R2-D2's booster rockets were originally intended to have debuted in *The Phantom Menace*. They would have featured in a scene in which the droid fell off a landing platform on Coruscant only to fly back to safety.

When Anakin slaughters the Tusken Raiders, the voice of Qui-Gon (Liam Neeson) can be heard shouting "No, Anakin!"

The Jedi who attempts to attack Count Dooku before Jango Fett shoots him down is Coleman Trebor. This is a reference to Rob Coleman, the effects supervisor on *Attack of the Clones*.

Just before he is killed by Mace Windu, Jango Fett can be seen trying to start his jetpack, which malfunctions. George Lucas added sparks—that were not originally present in the cinematic release— to the DVD version of the film.

Dexter Jettster's name is a reference to George Lucas' nickname for his son, Jett.

The story behind the mysterious Jedi Sifo-Dyas was later featured in a story arc in the sixth season of *Star Wars: The Clone Wars*.

Producer Rick McCallum cites *Attack of the Clones* as the prequel that was the hardest to make because everything was done digitally, from shooting to distribution.

A humorous documentary entitled *R2-D2: Beneath the Dome* was included with some home-release editions of the film.

According to visual effects supervisor John Knoll, Boba Fett remembers Obi-Wan's strategy of attaching his ship to an asteroid in order to escape sensors when Han Solo lands the *Millennium Falcon* on the side of the Star Destroyer.

Attack of the Clones features the first chronological use of John Williams' *The Imperial March*.

Scenes cut from the final version of the film include Anakin and Padmé spending time with her family on Naboo, Anakin and Padmé interrogated and put on trial by Poggle the Lesser on Geonosis, and the Jedi attacking a droid control ship.

A 3D presentation of *Attack of the Clones* was shown exclusively at the Celebration Europe II fan convention in July 2013.

STAR WARS

EPISODE III

REVENGE OF THE SITH

The final part of the *Star Wars* prequel trilogy, *Revenge of the Sith* marked the final piece of the puzzle as we learned why Anakin fell to the dark side and how a Republic became an Empire. For George Lucas, it marked the end of the big-screen story of how Anakin Skywalker became Darth Vader.

George Lucas (Writer/Director): *Star Wars* was intended to be one movie. You never saw what came before and you never saw what came after. It was designed to be the tragedy of Darth Vader, which starts with Darth Vader coming through the door and throwing everybody around. Halfway through the story, you realize he is actually a man and that the hero is his son. In the end, the villain turns into the hero because he is inspired by his son. I broke it up because I didn't have the money to do that and it would have been a five-hour movie. The icon of Darth Vader took over and his tragedy got diminished. It was harder to see that it was actually a story about a guy who is redeemed.

The backstory was written as a backstory, it wasn't intended to be a movie. Technically, we couldn't do it, because we were going to the center of the universe. *A New Hope* was designed, for technical reasons, to be on the edge of the universe, so I didn't have to deal with lots of costumes and special effects. After about ten years, I began to think it would be interesting to tell the full story of what happened and strengthen that part of it. At the same time, the technology became available for me to actually tell that story and visit the center of the universe that I'd had to avoid. I had a long, soul-searching time: Should I take one last shot at *Star Wars* and maybe tell the backstory so that the tragedy becomes more apparent? I thought I would regret it if I didn't do it.

2 /

Ewan McGregor (Obi-Wan Kenobi): In Episode I, we had a lot of work to do to establish the plot and set up the saga as a whole. In turn, Episode II was very melodramatic. Episode III is nonstop action!

George Lucas: There are no plot twists in this one. You know he turns into Darth Vader!

The film presented a challenge for stalwart costume designer Trisha Bigga as she dressed a galaxy of characters.

Trisha Biggar (Costume Designer): I began working on the project in August of 2002. At that time, I went to the Skywalker Ranch to have an initial meeting with George to talk about what he was envisioning for the various environments and to see what the concept artists had started developing for those environments.

3 /

1 / Hayden Christensen turns to the dark side as Anakin Skywalker. (Previous spread)

2 / George Lucas directs Samuel L. Jackson (Mace Windu).

3 / Bruce Spence lurks in the shadows as Tion Medon, a port administrator on Utapau.

I then returned to London to look at fabrics and to start thinking about colors and so forth.

For each planet and galaxy that is seen, we break down each story into days. For instance, on Coruscant, we would work out when it was morning, afternoon, evening or even the next day, and decide when to make a costume change. Usually, if it's the next day, [the actor] will get a change of clothes, unless there is a reason why they would be wearing the same costume. George has a very clear idea of what he wants—even if the script wasn't on paper, the storyline is in his head. George fancies costume changes.

One cast member did not get a costume upgrade.

Anthony Daniels (C-3PO): If you've met [producer] Rick McCallum, you know he's not about to pay for a new costume every time we do a new movie! I actually wore the same costume and it's beginning to smell a bit! I work out a bit to stay a little healthy, like Hayden Christensen.

The weirdest thing for me was talking to myself through most of these movies because R2-D2 is adorable, but he doesn't speak. It's hard to do a performance with characters who don't respond. I tried to get George to go "Beep!" at the end of each line I'd said. We were out in the desert and the camera was in the distance and I was yelling at him and he said "Oh, sure." So we did the scene again, and I said [*mimics C-3PO voice*] "Where are you going?"and seconds later I heard, "Oh! Beep!"

Attack of the Clones reunited Ewan McGregor with Hayden Christensen as they explored the highs and lows of Obi-Wan Kenobi and Anakin Skywalker's doomed friendship.

Ewan McGregor: Hayden and I actually created a relationship that mimicked our relationship ▶

4 /

6 /

<table>
</table>

offscreen. We got on terribly well. Obi-Wan and Anakin have a bond that needs to be there to make the original trilogy work.

In Episode I, Obi-Wan is wary of Anakin as a child. He only really trains him because he made a promise to his dying master, Qui-Gon. In Episode II, Obi-Wan is very wary for Anakin because I think he really loves him. When Anakin gives in to his anger or shows that his arrogance is getting in the way of him becoming a Jedi, Obi-Wan is disappointed for Anakin.

There's a scene where I've given a lecture about what's happening in a certain place during the Clone Wars, and Anakin comes in late. That scene sums up their relationship —Obi-Wan is disappointed *for* Anakin, not *with* him.

Hayden Christensen (Anakin Skywalker): Anakin and Obi-Wan regard each other as comrades. Their relationship has moved past the point of being teacher and student as Anakin has learned his craft. They share banter between one another, which makes watching

their relationship fall apart all the more devastating.

It took me by surprise when I read it in the script for the first time. But it was a necessary evil. All the Jedi had to go, what can I say? Even the children. It's a dark film, and Anakin does very dark things. Anakin is definitely the bad guy in this one. This was the time in Anakin's life that I had been looking forward to—making that dark transition to Darth Vader. There's just more fun to be had and more emotions to explore. I really enjoyed making this one.

The role of Anakin posed a unique challenge for Hayden Christensen as he provided the link between two very disparate versions of the Chosen One.

Hayden Christensen: Playing Anakin was a difficult challenge because I didn't have someone to emulate, like Ewan McGregor who had Alec Guinness. Yet I still had a character who was predefined by the other actors who played him. Ultimately, I had to be the linear connection between the Anakin that Jake

Lloyd played and Darth Vader. I also had to capture the Anakin played by Sebastian Shaw at the end of *Return of the Jedi*.

It's a daunting task taking on a role that has such attention. As much as possible, I tried to disregard all of it. There were a few very pivotal scenes that were difficult. Obviously, the fight between myself, Ian McDiarmid, and Samuel L. Jackson was a big one. Thankfully, George had conceived such a well-drawn character that all I had to do was follow the script.

The story picks up the bittersweet romance between Anakin and Padmé as Natalie Portman returned as the now pregnant senator, fighting for the soul of her Jedi husband.

Natalie Portman (Padmé): It was really exciting to do real, substantive scenes with Ewan McGregor. Our scenes together were problematic because the relationship between Padmé and Obi-Wan really developed between *Attack of the Clones* and *Revenge of the Sith*. In that time, they have become friends to the

4 / Ewan McGregor as Obi-Wan fights Grievous, before the background and the General elements were added.

5 / Obi-Wan Kenobi and his apprentice, Anakin Skywalker.

6 / Obi-Wan and Padmé discuss Anakin's evil deeds.

7 / Ewan McGregor in action as General Obi-Wan Kenobi.

▶ point where he feels comfortable telling her things that are very personal, dramatic, and life changing. So it was really interesting to go through the process of figuring out what we have been through to get to this point: Have we ever hung out alone? Have we only been friends through Anakin? Do we have a separate relationship apart from that?

Trisha Biggar: In *Revenge of the Sith*, Padmé's situation is more serious, and the colors [we used] are much darker and more muted—less playful. Now, there is a war going on and Anakin is away, nobody knows she's married, much less pregnant.

Natalie Portman: Trisha Biggar is an outstanding costume designer. The fabrics she used were incredible and the detail was amazing. She and [director of photography] David Tattersall had meetings about what the costumes would look like when they were filmed. The costumes caught the light in the most interesting ways that it seemed as if they were always changing. There's a peacock and brown dress that looked like a completely different color depending on the angle it was filmed.

David Tattersall (Director of Photography): Trisha would offer us fabrics for us to look at. We would hold them in front of different types of lights, hard and soft, and different colors to see how they worked best.

Natalie Portman: Padmé wouldn't have lost Anakin if she weren't so committed to the Republic. If she had a different concept of government or morality, she might have been able to stay with Anakin—if her loyalties to him were above everything else. Padmé is a pretty centered person so it's not like

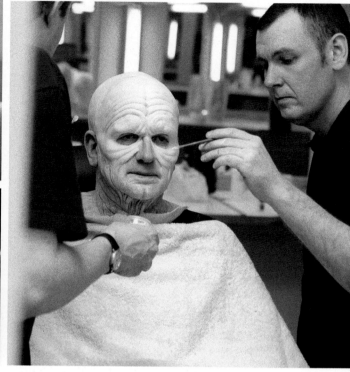

she's going through a big internal change; it's the external things that are changing around her and she has to cope with that.

Portman enjoyed playing the empowered leader who stays true to her beliefs.

Natalie Portman: I definitely appreciate the fact that the role defines the true meaning of feminism as I interpret it. Feminism is often misconstrued as women wanting to be like men.

True feminism for me is bringing out what is particular to women, because we are different. I think Padmé is an amazing example because she is a politician and a leader of many people. But rather than being consumed with a thirst for power as many of the people around her are, both men and women, she stays true to her compassion and belief in democracy and humanity. I think that's really important.

8 / Natalie Portman, dressed to meet Anakin after he has rescued Palpatine.

9 / Portman dons another Trisha Biggar creation.

10 / The Emperor strikes back at Yoda.

11 / Ian McDiarmid's evil transformation.

Returning as the charismatic Sith Lord, Count Dooku, Christopher Lee played a small yet pivotal role in a sequence that showed Anakin taking a big step to the dark side.

Christopher Lee (Count Dooku): Dooku means "poison" in Japanese, which is appropriate because he is lethal. But he is not simply a bad guy. He was good and then became bad. At one time, Dooku was a good man. He crossed over to become a Separatist because he was disgusted with the way the Republic was functioning. He obviously holds very strong beliefs. And maybe at one time he was right—maybe the Republic was corrupt, and he decided he didn't want to become corrupt himself. So he started his own group. Then, of course it became a war. Everyone has a dark side —everyone. The important thing is to make sure the dark side doesn't overpower the light side.

Dooku makes the switch on his own accord—nobody makes him do it—which is different from

Anakin. Anakin does so without knowing it or even wanting it and becomes enmeshed in a trap by Palpatine. There is a lust for power that initially emanates from the Emperor who is very corrupt himself. What was he like when he was a young man? Who knows? Not many people are corrupt from the moment they're born—it does take a bit of time.

Hayden Christensen: Christopher Lee is full of stories. What a man! He is a well of knowledge and experience. He's very happy to share it all. I always tried to sit down with him whenever I could and get a story out of him.

Coming to the forefront as his plans come to fruition is Palpatine, known as Darth Sidious, played by Ian McDiarmid.

Ian McDiarmid: I just played a straightforward politician—now there's a contradiction in terms! Palpatine is charming, smiling, out ▶

12 /

for the good of the universe, and its community. But underneath there lurks a monster, so it was very easy to build the character; I just looked in the newspapers!

However, the true face of Palpatine emerges as Darth Sidious is revealed.

Ian McDiarmid: It certainly helps to be a monster in monster's makeup. But George was very interesting when we started shooting *The Phantom Menace*. He said, "You should think of your eyes as his contact lenses," which is a great thing to say to an actor. My face was actually his mask and then when I put on the mask, I become him. So that kind of schizophrenia was always fun to play, and in this film, it's great because one explodes through the other, and now he is who he is. This is when the true person comes out, letting the evil fully manifest itself.

The Emperor that you see in *Return of the Jedi* looks like he does because he's very old and evil—it is what he always looked like. He just had the carapace of looking like a fairly ordinary guy, a politician who smiled a bit and so on.

I don't think George had made up his mind, when we started shooting, whether to continually show Palpatine as he really is after the initial transformation or if Sidious would go back and forth with his appearance. I think that when George saw Dave Elsey's wonderful makeup, he decided that constantly going back and forth would be a step back.

Trisha Biggar: [Stunt costumes] have to be detailed very closely to the original costumes. For Palpatine's stunt costume, we used exactly the same fabric as we did for [Ian McDiarmid's costumes]—they are complete copies. In that case, we allowed for extra padding to be worn underneath by the stunt man.

13 /

12 / Palpatine and his aides, Mas Amedda (David Bowers) and Sly Moore (Sandi Finlay).

13 / Palpatine faces off against Mace Windu in a fight to the death.

14 / George Lucas talks actors, Kenji Oates (Saesee Tiin) and Samuel L. Jackson, through a scene.

15 / Palpatine seduces Anakin with the tale of Darth Plagueis the Wise.

Ian McDiarmid: I found that when I read the script, not only did I have a lot to say, I also had a lot to do! Palpatine had turned into an action man. I knew we would be shooting the fight scenes in about five days, so I didn't have long to get up to speed. Michael Burn, a brilliant stunt double who does most of my fight work, got up to speed for me! My opponent, Samuel L. Jackson, was an extremely proficient swordsman and very helpful and understanding when I made mistakes.

Hayden Christensen: I was able to work with Ian McDiarmid a little bit on *Attack of the Clones* but because our relationship really

grows in *Revenge of the Sith*, we were able to work together more. It was more than a pleasure to go to work and have such a learning experience. He was always open about having a dialogue about the work and wanting to talk about the subtext of what was being played. His character is so dark and evil, yet he just goes in and out of it with such ease that it was amazing to watch. I can't do that. Ian really steals the show in this film.

Ian McDiarmid: Anakin doesn't have a father—or if he does we don't know who he is. *Revenge of the Sith* doesn't provide any definitive clues, leaving the whole

area ambiguous. There are a few clues dotted around and if anyone wanted to join the dots then they can. What I liked about this film is that there isn't a revelatory fact—there are just a few possibilities.

Hayden Christensen: I loved the scenes where he did most of the talking. There were a couple of times where I just nodded my head and agreed with the story he was telling me. Also, there's the scene where Ian and I are at the opera,

and he's telling me about another master and apprentice where the apprentice overthrows the master and takes all his powers. That was one of those scenes where I would lose my place because of the manner in which he was telling the story and getting his point across.

Ian McDiarmid: The main day for my part of the fight was also the day we filmed the big scene between Hayden and me at the theater. The scene was originally supposed to be in Palpatine's

office, but George thought it would be more interesting putting it into a box of the theater and he was right. Palpatine's one redeemable feature is that he is a patron of the arts! That was my biggest dialogue scene and that was shot at 4:20 p.m. on a Friday afternoon after I had been fighting all day. I can honestly say that week—involving those dialogue scenes, the fight, and wearing the prosthetic—was the most challenging of my acting life.

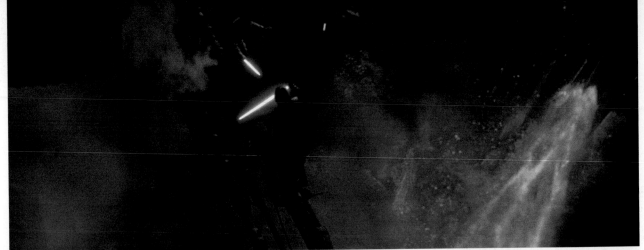

▶ The film demanded much from the main actors as they picked up lightsabers for some of the most spectacular fights in the saga.

Hayden Christensen: Learning the moves wasn't that difficult. Nick Gillard really outdid himself for this film and choreographed a pretty spectacular fight. Ewan and I trained together and laughed all the while. I just couldn't wait to shoot the final duel. Ewan and I would even escape the business and chaos of what was happening on set by stepping aside and grabbing a couple of lightsabers and practicing our fight.

The repetitiveness of having to do each scene again and again for all the different camera angles —while trying to make each take as perfect as possible—was exhausting. It was difficult at times because it was so hot and the

costumes weren't really conducive to the footing. We'd often get tangled up in our own costumes, which was aggravating. But at the same time, we were fighting with lightsabers, so it was like being a kid causing a ruckus and breaking a sweat!

Ewan McGregor: There's an enormous amount of fighting and it starts right after the opening crawl with a sequence that in the first cut lasted about thirty-five minutes. Because it was the last film of the trilogy, we really pulled out the stops—there were no holds barred this time!

Samuel L. Jackson: I felt pretty great about dying in *Revenge of the Sith*. It's a satisfying death. From the time I was two or three years old, my friends would swordfight with sticks. It's almost

like I practiced for this death scene all my life!

Nick Gillard and I have been talking about my fight against Palpatine for a couple of years, and he graciously has been trying to figure out a really wonderful lightsaber battle for me to do. He combined a lot of different fighting styles, so it looks very good. It's spectacular and shows off my skills. It shows many sides of Mace; it makes him look dominant and makes him look vulnerable. It makes him sneaky and makes him look strong. Mace is very at ease, yet very lethal. I had to learn ninety-seven moves in two or three days. I then had to learn how to speed up the moves and move at the same time.

Ewan McGregor: I'm very happy with all the fighting scenes, even though they were incredibly

16 / The Jedi battle it out on Mustafar.

17 / As Palpatine issues Order 66, Yoda fights for his life against his former allies.

18 / The Emperor's royal guards arrive.

exhausting to do. Hayden and I were constantly filming each sequence at such a fast pace. We would film one scene right after the other.

The fights were very slow-going now that I'm a bit older than when I filmed Episode I. For that film, I'd fight all day long. I didn't care. Whereas now, it's like, "Okay guys, I think that's it. I've reached my limit." At first, my movements looked very wooden and it took about two weeks for my style to come back because my body had to remember what it was like. There was an enormous number of moves to learn, and none of the fighting was improvised. We had to perform each move so quickly, we didn't have time to think about them. Because we were moving so quickly, our bodies had to remember where the next cut was coming from. We weren't thinking, *Okay, he's coming*

to my shoulder, now he's going to cut my head. It all had to be fluid.

Ian McDiarmid: I couldn't wait to see Palpatine as a big-action villain, which he's now turned into because he has two rather impressive lightsaber fights. I really enjoyed fighting Yoda. It's two masters of good and evil having a confrontation.

The movie's climatic battle was a fight that had been long-awaited since it was first alluded to in the original 1977 movie as Obi-Wan and Anakin clashed sabers.

Ewan McGregor: Right up to the end, I think Obi-Wan still had hope that Anakin would come back from the dark side. However, there's a certain point where he realizes that there is no hope and the cloak comes off.

Hayden Christensen: It was important to Nick Gillard that he installed a story to the fight to show an exchange of power. My character is meant to be the Chosen One and I'm supposed to be one of the better Jedi as far as fighting goes, yet I come out in the short end of it. Nick balanced the fight perfectly so neither Ewan nor I look substantially weaker than the other.

I had a scene where Nick plays a Jedi instructor who Anakin kills. We had so much fun with it. I clipped him right in the forehead with my lightsaber, which was a total accident. He thinks it was intentional, but I didn't mean to do it! In the next take, he smacked me in the head and got me back.

Nick Gillard: There is a lot of fighting in this film—almost forty percent of the film—and the end ▶

19 / Hayden Christensen is made-up to show Anakin's injuries.

20 / Makeup maestro Dave Elsey works on Hayden Christensen.

► battle is very long. I believe the two combatants travel a quarter of a mile during the fight and they perform more than 800 moves. There's no dialogue during the fight except for three lines, so it was very important that the swordplay acted as the dialogue.

The explosion of the fight means that the first three or four minutes contains all the flashy moves. After that explosion, we had to figure out what it would be like for two people to fight who know each other so well —it's like fighting yourself. We did loads of sections where neither man could get through to the other—they matched each other's moves. Obi-Wan doesn't really want to kill Anakin. In the end, Anakin makes a mistake by getting too angry and Obi-Wan doesn't make mistakes.

Defeated by his former master, Anakin's transformation to the dark side is completed as he is trapped in the oppressive armor of Darth Vader.

Ian McDiarmid: Anakin doesn't want to do bad things but he's persuadable, as we saw in *Attack of the Clones* in his understandable overaction to what happened to his mother. This is something that Palpatine uses; in some vague way, he may even have been responsible for it.

Palpatine has arranged everything in *Revenge of the Sith* except that final duel between Anakin and Obi-Wan. He finds Anakin near death and, like all arch-political pragmatists, he converts a seeming tragedy into an opportunity and rebuilds him as this huge, unsympathetic metal creature, thereby creating the greatest villain of all time —next to himself, of course. Palpatine wanted Anakin, the greatest warrior ever, to protect the Empire.

Hayden Christensen: The prosthetic makeup was good fun for me! It wasn't the most comfortable thing but it was

20 /

great to act in. I only had to be in it for one day. It was liberating to not have to see myself, and I got to change my voice a little so I didn't have to hear myself either. Having to take it off was a nightmare. They glued every inch to my skin, so that it would move with my expressions. I think I lost a layer of skin taking it off.

Ian McDiarmid: I was pleased that when Anakin is almost brutally destroyed, Palpatine is relived to not only find him alive but also because he is Anakin Skywalker. There is one moment that George scripted in a rather casual way where I touch Anakin's forehead. I think that's really the

only human moment we see from Palpatine—just a moment of sympathy and compassion for another human being. Not the usual ingredients of the Sith.

One of the highlights of Hayden Christensen's experience making two *Star Wars* films was putting on the Darth Vader suit for the final scenes of the film.

Hayden Christensen: It was a thrilling moment, lying there on the operating table as that mask came into frame. And then putting on the full Darth Vader suit was something I had been looking forward to since I found out I got the part. The costume

department made a brand-new Darth Vader suit. They were really nice to allow me to get into the Darth Vader suit because they could have just put some really tall guy into it. I begged and pleaded! They had to make a big muscle suit, like one of those sumo wrestler suits that you get into at the fair, so that I would fill the costume out. The costume team put a little breathing apparatus on the costume so when I came out, it felt like the whole Darth Vader.

You'd think putting that suit on would be pretty empowering, but it was really quite the opposite. I didn't really have any peripheral vision, so my sight ▶

21 /

22 /

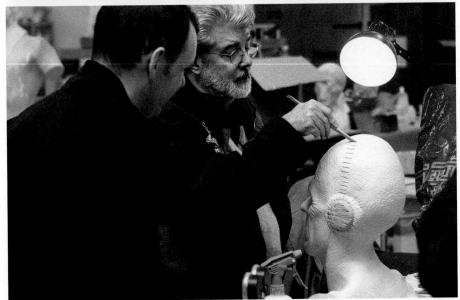

was limited. Plus, all the sound around me was muffled, which made me feel quite disoriented. It was a heavy costume and I was walking around in five-inch stilts to compensate for the height difference. It was definitely not the most comfortable thing to have to spend more than ten minutes in. It was really hot and kind of like putting hydrogen peroxide on a cut. There was a fair amount of staring when I first emerged as Vader. For me, it was more about trying to stay on my feet, keep the sweat out of my eyes, and make it up the stairs without falling over! I just kept picturing how mad everyone would be if I tripped and scuffed the helmet or something. At the same time, it was quite something to stand next to Darth Sidious and say the lines. Even though my voice was replaced by James Earl Jones, it felt good to say the dialogue.

Trisha Biggar (Costume Designer): We didn't make any major changes [to the Darth Vader costume] at all, except we made the costume fit Hayden Christensen—it's completely new. There are some things that we've [corrected] however, like the helmet —the original was completely uneven. When it was first sculpted, it was obviously done by hand, and one side of the face is slightly at an angle. We made it so that it was symmetrical. It allowed Hayden a lot of extra head movement that wasn't possible before.

Hayden Christensen: I was always curious as to what Darth Vader looks like under the mask and now I know he looks like me!

The final shot of the film echoed an iconic scene from *A New Hope*.

Bonnie Piesse (Beru): The final scene was the first time I ever worked with a green screen. It was

extremely odd little time jump. The last line isn't the most Shakespearean of lines, it's, "Oh no!" Jimmy Smits [Bail Organa] said, "How can I say this? How can I have this droid's memory wiped just like that?" I just replied, "Think of him as a washing machine, he's a household object. He doesn't feel."

Samuel L. Jackson: Everyone sees something different inside these films. Such as the heroic, societal, and political aspects. The story itself is one we all know; it's like all morality tales, the good vs evil kind of thing. But it's still kind of tongue in cheek because it's hard to tell what is good and bad—you get to make your own choices about that. As I read the story for Episode III, I felt the Shakespearian aspects would cause a lot of debate among people. In the end, I love the way it all plays out.

George knows his audiences, and he cares about them. He cares about the kids; kids need stories that are for and about them.

Christopher Lee: *Star Wars* is the ultimate in filmmaking and film viewing for millions of people the world over. In many ways, it is like a Shakespearean tragedy. Don't forget that, eventually, good triumphs over evil.

John Williams: It was one of my great ambitions in life to complete this journey with George, step by step.

George Lucas: The first film is always the toughest, because you don't know what's going on, and you have to learn as you go! Everything is a drama and it drives you nuts. Then, you have the next one, and the next one, and each time it gets easier and easier because you learn what to expect. When you get to the last one, it's a piece of cake. It's very much like that with the movies. The first was definitely the hardest and the last one was definitely the easiest. ☻

kind of like playing make believe. I walked out onto the set and Joel Edgerton (Owen Lars) wasn't there! He filmed his part in Ireland many months later, so they had a stand-in for him. George said to me, "Imagine epic music playing as you stare out at this amazing sunset!" My eyeline was actually a broomstick!

For Lucas, *Revenge of the Sith* marked an end of his overseeing the *Star Wars* movies, though it certainly wasn't the end of the saga.

George Lucas: It's like having your kids going off to college. They still come back when they need money! They'll be there for holidays. We're doing the TV shows, so it's still going to be around. Now it's on its own, it's going to be doing its own thing, but I reserved the theatrical arena for this saga, which started out as a two-hour idea and turned into a twelve-hour idea!

Ewan McGregor: I had a couple of moments while filming *Revenge of the Sith* that have taken me back to my childhood and both have been filming with Anthony Daniels. Being on set with C-3PO made me remember what it was like to be seven years old and watching the original films. I felt the excitement of being in the prequels now. I was also in a scene with R2-D2, which was weird as I found myself quite choked up about this droid!

Anthony Daniels: I didn't realize that I had the last line in *Revenge of the Sith* because the script can often change. I had the first line of the first movie, which was, "Did you hear that? They shut down the main reactor. There'll be no escape for the princess this time!" I didn't really know what I was talking about! I'd never been in a film before and I thought, *This is weird*. George and I, twenty-eight years later, walked onto the sound-stage in Australia and saw the same set and it was an

21 / Hayden Christensen on set as Darth Vader confers with his true master, George Lucas!

22 / George Lucas gets hands on, showing Dave Elsey what an Utapaun should look like.

23 / Filming the last scene of the movie in the studio before the desert is added as a background.

24 / Grand Moff Tarkin makes a surprise appearance during the closing moments of the film.

STAR WARS
EPISODE III
REVENGE OF THE SITH

STAR WARS   EPISODE III   REVENGE OF THE SITH

Starring EWAN McGREGOR   NATALIE PORTMAN   HAYDEN CHRISTENSEN

IAN McDIARMID   SAMUEL L. JACKSON   CHRISTOPHER LEE

Co-starring ANTHONY DANIELS   KENNY BAKER   FRANK OZ
Music by JOHN WILLIAMS   Produced by RICK McCALLUM

Written and Directed by
GEORGE LUCAS

Special Visual Effects and Animation by INDUSTRIAL LIGHT & MAGIC
A LUCASFILM LTD. Production · A TWENTIETH CENTURY FOX Release
Soundtrack Available on SONY CLASSICAL   Read the Novel from DEL REY BOOKS
www.starwars.com

STAR WARS: REVENGE OF THE SITH

ESSENTIAL TRIVIA

In her book *Glittering Images*, art critic Camille Paglia named George Lucas as the greatest artist of our time. She cited the duel on Mustafar as his masterpiece.

The film features cameo appearances from Jeremy Bulloch (as Captain Colton), and the Lucas family: George Lucas (as Baron Papanoida), Katie Lucas (as Chi Eekway Papanoida), Amanda Lucas (as Terr Taneel), and Jett Lucas (as Zett Jukassa).

Originally planned for the first *Star Wars* movie, the battle on Kashyyyk is our first and only big-screen visit to the Wookiee homeworld.

The Jedi Shaak Ti was originally scripted to be killed by General Grievous. Although the scene was shot, it was deleted from the final cut of the film.

Steven Spielberg assisted in the previsulization of the film, notably in the duels between Obi-Wan and Anakin, and Yoda and Palpatine. He also oversaw the animatic of an extended chase on Utapau between Obi-Wan and General Grievous.

At the end of Obi-Wan and Anakin's duel, Obi-Wan picks his fallen apprentice's lightsaber up from the ground. This lightsaber is then given to Luke in *A New Hope*.

The sound of General Grievous's cough in the film is George Lucas' own cough that he suffered with during production.

When Anakin, Obi-Wan, and Palpatine land in the transport ship, a YT-3000-class ship similar to the *Millennium Falcon* can briefly be seen docking.

Aiden Barton played both Luke *and* Leia as babies. He is the son of editor Roger Barton.

Actress Genevieve O'Reilly filmed scenes as Mon Mothma which were cut from the final edit. However, she was eventually seen on screen as the character in *Rogue One: A Star Wars Story*.

A scene showing Yoda arriving on Dagobah in his ship was deleted from the final cut of the film.

Peter Mayhew reprised his role as Chewbacca for the first time since *Return of the Jedi*.

Revenge of the Sith is the only film in the prequel trilogy to feature C-3PO in his gold casing.

During the battle of Kashyyyk, a swinging Wookiee emits a "Tarzan" yell, echoing the same yell when Chewbacca swings onto the AT-ST in *Return of the Jedi*.

This is the only movie in the saga in which Darth Sidious wields a lightsaber.

In an early draft of the screenplay, a young Han Solo was to have been revealed to be living among the Wookiees.

A line in which Palpatine reveals that Dooku paid the Tusken Raiders to kidnap and torture Shmi Skywalker to death was cut from the final film.

An early piece of concept art for the film featured General Grievous as a child sat in a floating chair with two IG-88 droids as bodyguards.

Revenge of the Sith was the first *Star Wars* movie to get a PG-13 rating.

Revenge of the Sith was the first *Star Wars* film not to be widely released on VHS.

When Obi-Wan leaps down to face General Grievous, he says, "Hello there!" This is also his first line in *A New Hope*.

The images of the volcanic eruptions on Mustafar utilized real life footage of the eruption of Mount Etna in Italy.

Several basketball players were cast as Wookiees in *Revenge of the Sith* after the casting team put out a call to Australian basketball teams looking for "taller than tall guys."

The movie features a blockade runner similar to the *Tantive IV*.

James Earl Jones, Ian McDiarmid, Kenny Baker, Anthony Daniels, Frank Oz, and Peter Mayhew are the only actors to feature in the original and prequel trilogies.

THE ORIGINAL TRILOGY

1977–1983

STAR WARS
A NEW HOPE

A triumph of the imagination of George Lucas, *Star Wars: A New Hope* introduced the world to iconic characters such as Darth Vader, Luke Skywalker, and Princess Leia and, as the intital teaser trailer proclaimed, "aliens from a thousand worlds." The film brought together a cast ranging from established screen actors such as Sir Alec Guinness and Peter Cushing to virtual unknowns, Carrie Fisher, Harrison Ford, and Mark Hamill.

Mark Hamill (Luke Skywalker): [Before joining the *Star Wars* cast], I wanted to be in *Apocalypse Now* (1979). Fred Roos [casting director] had a lot to do with guiding George Lucas in my direction. I think George did say he was doing a science-fiction film. I had seen *American Graffiti* (1973) three or four times. I didn't see *THX 1138* (1971) until after I had made *Star Wars*. I also saw the student film at a science-fiction convention that we went to.

But I was amazed how perfectly constructed the story of *Star Wars* is. Luke grows up in *Star Wars*. He's thrown into this thing, but he learns a whole lot. There was also that romantic triangle. It's like Cary Grant, Rosalind Russell, and Ralph Bellamy in *His Girl Friday* (1940). The two robots, Artoo-Detoo and See-Threepio, are like Laurel and Hardy. I love them. I think they are my favorite pair of characters in the movie. I enjoy Harrison Ford's character, Han Solo, the most. But then I think Luke Skywalker also emulates Han, so we're getting into how there are parallels between the cast and the storyline.

Carrie Fisher (Princess Leia Organa): It was always assumed that I would [act], so I kind of went along with that assumption. For a very short time, I did want to be a teacher. I also wanted to be a stewardess, so I could travel; I don't know why, because I hate planes—although I can't hate them too much because I fly around a lot. But mostly, I always wanted to act.

Alec Guinness (Ben "Obi-Wan" Kenobi): I'm just grateful for any work that comes along. You know, I have to pay the rent like everybody else!

Mark Hamill: Sir Alec is my favorite actor. I think there's nobody more versatile than he is. A lot of people can't identify him, he looks different in all of his movies. As a kid, I loved *The Lavender Hill Mob* (1951) and *The Ladykillers* (1955). Those were my favorites. I was completely in awe of the guy. But he's so humble and so disinterested in himself, it's amazing. He doesn't consider himself an important figure in cinema. He doesn't like to talk about his movies, he doesn't think they are important. He's more thrilled at getting nominated for his screenplay, for *The Horse's Mouth* (1958). That was more important to him.

Alec Guinness: George Lucas had very little to say during the filming. He simply sensed when you were uncomfortable, walked across and dropped a brief word in your ear. Good actors don't like to be told how to act.

Peter Mayhew (Chewbacca): Sir Alec was very good. He was a true professional. If anything went wrong with his performance, if he screwed up on a line or a look, he'd apologize to everybody and go back and do it again. When he wasn't working, he was a very nice man to sit down and talk to because he had so many fascinating stories and observations about theater, films, and his long, distinguished career.

Adding comic relief, and forming a through-line that would extend to all nine films in the saga are the droids, C-3PO and R2-D2, brought to life by Anthony Daniels and Kenny Baker.

Anthony Daniels (C-3PO): I spent some months in Elstree with a team of plasterers and a lovely sculptor called Liz Moore. First they covered every part of me in Vaseline and then cling-film. It was a rather disgusting experience! Then they put together a statue of me cast from the molds they created. Liz then used clay to build up a design you see on the screen. She was very good, but it wasn't until I saw a picture of myself on the first day's shooting in Tunisia that I knew what I was playing for the next twelve weeks.

Kenny Baker (R2-D2): My costume weighs about eighty pounds and is quite heavy and I couldn't phsyically move it, apart from wobbling and jerking it around and moving the head.

1 / Mark Hamill surveys the sandcrawler, under construction on location in Tunisia. (Previous spread)

2 / George Lucas directs Carrie Fisher and Mark Hamill as they make their escape from the Death Star.

3 / Peter Cushing, a stalwart of the Hammer series of horror films, lent a touch of menace as Grand Moff Tarkin.

4 / Stunt man Peter Diamond, Sir Alec Guinness, and George Lucas on set for Obi-Wan's last stand.

5 / Laugh it up! Peter Mayhew, Harrison Ford, and Mark Hamill clown around on set.

6 / Ultimately deleted from the intitial cut of the movie, Han's encounter with Jabba the Hutt (at this point played by Declan Mulholland) would later be reinstated thanks to the wonders of CGI. (Overleaf)

4 /

5 /

Anthony Daniels: Threepio has my voice, with a tiny amount of echo added to make him sound tinny. I feel a bit self-concious talking like Threepio unless I'm in the suit. Luke and Han sound like Mark and Harrison on set, but I had to accept that talking like Threepio left myself open to some odd looks, especially from Harrison.

Although he had worked with George Lucas on the director's acclaimed 1973 movie *American Graffiti*, Harrison Ford's performance as the smooth-talking scoundrel Han Solo arguably made him a star. In *Star Wars*, he formed part of an iconic double act with Chewbacca, a towering Wookiee played with humor and sensitivity by Peter Mayhew. He also has a sparky relationship with Carrie Fisher's Princess Leia.

Harrison Ford (Han Solo): The princess is the product of her own world, and has her own intelligence and wit. There's no

▶ doubt about it that it's the same for all of us. It's built in. A certain amount of your behavior is based on accepting your environment and a certain amount is based on a resistance to those things you want to change. Her cynicism about her environment is what makes her the right kind of princess for the movie.

Peter Mayhew: It was wonderful because [Harrison and I] were both about the same age. We both knew what our characters were. You don't do three movies playing closest buddies without some of it rubbing off a little bit.

Harrison Ford: There are laughs in *Star Wars*. I don't think there are jokes. The jokes are sort of in that long chase through the Death Star. There are lots of physical jokes in there.

While *Star Wars* was the vision of one man, George Lucas hired the best people to help realize the galaxy far far away. One of the earliest employees was Ralph McQuarrie, a former designer for the Boeing Company, who remarkably made his debut as a conceptual artist for film with *Star Wars*.

Ralph McQuarrie (conceptual artist): I did sketches just to illustrate the central idea. The general look and leg-wrapping thing for Luke came from a sketch I had done. The stormtroopers were definitely mine. I made the biggest contribution from a design point of view, simply because, at first, I was the only designer working on it. There were things like Darth Vader's mask, which evolved from concerns I had about him dying on the way between the two spaceships [in the draft that McQuarrie was initially working ▶

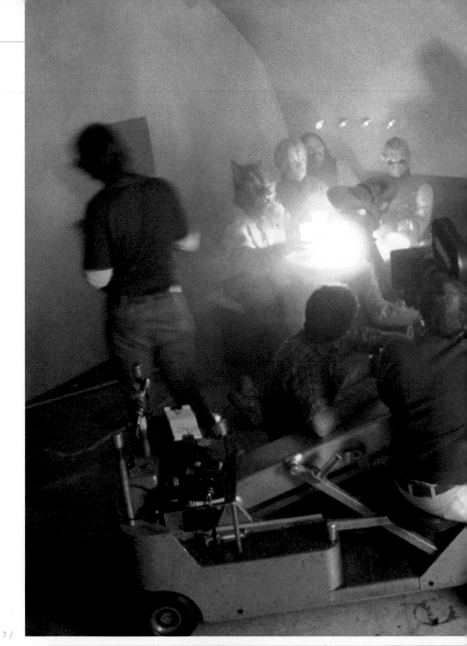

7 /

8 /

9 /

7 / George Lucas directs a closeup of some of the Mos Eisley cantina's patrons.

8 / Phil Brown and Mark Hamill bond on set.

9 / Anthony Daniels enjoys some refreshment while filming in the scorching Tunisian desert.

10 / George Lucas directs the ill-fated bounty hunter, Greedo.

11 / Chewbacca gets a brush up, courtesy of make-up artist Kathleen Freeborn.

12 / Luke, and his friends, together for one last time, in a scene that was cut from the final edit. (Overleaf)

10 /

11 /

on, Vader descends through space to attack the *Tantive IV*]. I don't think he thought we would keep the mask on him all through the picture. In the end, it was logical for him to keep the mask on for the whole picture. Why take it off, when there could be a mysterious reason for him to wear it, which nobody needed to know about?

Filming the strange space movie at Elstree Studios (in the U.K.) led to many of the British crew wondering what on earth it was that they were working on.

Harrison Ford: I didn't really notice any difference [between U.S. and U.K. crews]. The English crews are real democratic. They don't seem to be as "star oriented" as American crews can sometimes be. They treat everybody just about the same and are really pleasant. I don't think that they understood what was going on for a long time. They didn't know what it was that we were acting in and why. They didn't know whether it was some kind of comic book or what. They had no way of knowing that the movie was operating on several levels at the same time, because it's such an American kind of tale. I think it was the humor they didn't quite see.

13 / Luke ignites his father's lightsaber, which has yet to have its glow added by ILM.

14 / The crew prepare Luke's X-wing as it departs from the rebel base on Yavin 4.

15 / R2-D2 goes it alone—with the help of the crew! (Overleaf)

To face the film's heroes, Lucas created a character that would ultimately go down as one of the greatest cinematic villains of all time: The mysterious Sith Lord, Darth Vader, voiced by James Earl Jones, performed by David Prowse and clad in a costume sculpted by Brian Muir.

James Earl Jones: I was basically hired as a special effect. David Prowse was the guy acting as Darth Vader, okay? Why take that away from him? I got paid $7,000 for only two hours work. So to me, that was like I was rolling in a bunch of clover. Of course,

at the time, I did not know that if I had asked for percentage points of the gross, I would have been a millionaire overnight.

Brian Muir (sculpter, Darth Vader costume): The process started with David Prowse being molded from head to toe so that a full plaster cast could be produced for me to work on. As the mask and helmet were to be sculpted first, the head and shoulders were cut from the body and fixed onto a modeling stand. I began by sculpting the mask, back and front, ensuring that there was at least a quarter inch of clay on the plaster head at any point to allow for casting thickness, and to be sure it would fit well on Dave's head. After creating Vader's mask in clay, it was passed to the plasterers to mold and reproduce in plaster. I then carved and sharpened the plaster cast to a finish. At this point, I started modeling the helmet in clay

over the plaster mask to ensure the overall appearance worked. The same methods of molding and casting in plaster were again carried out. The final molds were made from the plaster cast, and fiberglass versions were produced. The plaster head and shoulders were then reaffixed to the body and it was moved to the main plaster shop for me to model the armor. Working from Ralph McQuarrie's paintings, I sculpted the chest armor, two shoulder bells, and shins. Again each piece was molded and cast in plaster, the lines carved and sharpened with a final remold, and cast in fiberglass.

David Prowse (Darth Vader): On the very first shot we did, I had to walk up a corridor. The camera was following me on a track going all the way up the corridor. I had decided that Vader would have a brisk, purposeful stride, meaning

that everybody had to trot quickly beside me to keep up. I strode to the end of the corridor and George said, "Sorry David, you've got to slow down. The camera can't keep up with you."

Darth Vader wasn't the main antagonist for this film, however. Lucas cast a veteran of cinematic evil-doing to play the commanding officer of the dreaded Death Star.

Peter Cushing (Grand Moff Tarkin): George Lucas knew his subject matter, and the effects were an eye-opener. An actor must think of his part and try to do it to the best of his ability, but the director must think of the technical side, which George did. I was knocked for six when I saw the film at the premiere. I was riveted. *Star Wars* was a picture you had to see again to take in what you missed the first time.

▶

PANAFLEX 21

1974	THE WIND AND THE LION
1974	FRENCH CONNECTION II
1975	THE MAN WHO WOULD BE KING
1975	YOU ARE MY DESTINY
1975	THE NEW SPARTANS
1975	THE SECRET LIFE OF PLANTS
1976	THE STAR WARS

"
I remember asking George [Lucas], 'Why am I living with my aunt and uncle? What happened to my mom and dad?'
"

Mark Hamill

▶ The film was produced by George Lucas' frequent collaborator, Gary Kurtz.

Mark Hamill: Gary and George are both so unique. You can't really compare them to any other producer-director you work with. Gary is a kid, too. The first time I really made a connection with Gary was in Tunisia. He gets this excited little grin that he sort of suppresses and tells you all about Scrooge McDuck and the island of PagoPago, or whatever.

He's really a partner with George. I've worked more closely with the producer on this than on anything. He's really accessible. They both are. You can walk up to them and ask them questions. There is no fear of intimidation there. There is not a power thing in it.

16 / Carrie Fisher as Princess Leia.

17 / Garrick Hagon goes before the cameras as Biggs takes to his X-wing.

18 / X-wing pilots and rebel troops enjoy a well-earned lunch break!

We're all in it together. I think George is really flexible about letting me try things. I mean, a lot of times you wouldn't even tell him what you were changing and you would do things and he wouldn't say anything. Whether he knows you're doing it or not, I don't know.

He told me not to say "THX 1138" anymore. We were bringing in the Wookiee, he's handcuffed, and the guy says, "Where are you going with this thing?" And the line was something like, "It's a prisoner transferred from cell block...." And then lots of letters and numbers. I love in-jokes, so I said, "This is prisoner transfer from THX 1138." He came over and said, "Don't do that." But we did four more takes and by the end I was doing it again. I think I did it on one he printed! With explosions and everything else involved, I just kept doing it.

The film was a real risk for Lucas, with the creation of the now-legendary visual effects studio eating into a large chunk of the small budget.

Paul Hirsch (editor): I remember George showed up one day with a plastic core in his hand, with a piece of film about ten feet long wrapped around it. The actual usable footage on it was around two or three seconds. "This cost a million dollars," he announced. It was the first shot produced by

ILM. The million dollars he referred to was the start-up cost of getting ILM off the ground. It was of a pair of laser cannons on the surface of the Death Star firing.

George Lucas' risk ultimately paid off... and then some, as talk turned to a sequel.

Carrie Fisher: Star Wars was an introduction. The relationships between the main characters were being established. It was made, I think, as a film to be cut. We would shoot a scene and then make any needed changes.

Joe Johnston: (effects illustration and design): [Star Wars] blew everything away. The start of the film caught the audience off guard. The whole opening sequence was George's idea; he knew exactly how he wanted it to work.

Mark Hamill: I was peppering George with questions all the time. All that extraneous minutiae that fans revel in was just dripping from every pore in my body. *What planet does a Wookiee come from? Where did Chewbacca learn how to fly a starship?* And I remember asking George, "Why am I living with my aunt and uncle? What happened to my mom and dad?" He made up lies, because he couldn't really tell me what was in store.... ☺

STAR WARS: A NEW HOPE

ESSENTIAL TRIVIA

George Lucas asked the crew to watch four films to prepare for working on *Star Wars*. They were: *2001: A Space Odyssey* (1968), *Silent Running* (1972), *Once Upon a Time in the West* (1968), and *Satyricon* (1969).

The opening crawl celebrates the Rebel Alliance's "First victory against the galactic Empire," an event not shown until *Rogue One: A Star Wars Story*.

C-3PO's panic while buried under a pile of wires was to have taken place aboard the *Tantive IV*. The shot eventually found a place later in the film, during the *Millennium Falcon*'s shoot-out with the Imperial TIE fighters.

The fate of the *Tantive IV* is not revealed in the movie, but the ship makes a return appearance in *The Rise of Skywalker*.

In the third draft of the screenplay, the Sand People attach bracelets to Luke's wrists and leave him suspended ten feet in the air. This is similar to Count Dooku's method of caging Obi-Wan in *Attack of the Clones*.

Regular sandtroopers wear black shoulder pauldrons, while patrol leaders wear orange ones. A similar ranking scheme appears in *The Phantom Menace*, where colored trim is used to distinguish the battle droids.

Kurt Russell, Christopher Walken, and Perry King were all considered for the role of Han Solo.

Close examination of Docking Bay 94 will allow you to make out the a stylized "94" on the walls.

After Tarkin snaps. "Terminate her immediately," the movie omits Darth Vader's scripted response, "And lose your only link to the rebel base? She can still be of value to us." Also cut from the film was Tarkin's comeback, "You'll get nothing more out of her. I'll find that hidden fortress if I have to destroy every star system in this sector!" This is a direct reference to Akira Kurosawa's *Hidden Fortress* (1958), a film George Lucas is known to admire.

Effects illustrator and designer Joe Johnston appears in an uncredited role as an Imperial gunner.

The tentacled trash monster, known as the dianoga, got its name from early outlines of the script which referred to "Dai Noga" warriors.

Mark Hamill and Carrie Fisher completed the rope swing across the Death Star chasm on their first try, without stunt doubles.

Because the crew didn't want to damage the expensive yak-fur costume, Chewbacca spent the entire trash compactor scene perched on a platform in the far corner.

The first character to say "May the Force be with you" on screen is General Dodonna, as he finishes his briefing to the rebel pilots as they are about to leave Yavin.

Although Chewbacca does not receive a medal alongside Luke and Han in *A New Hope*, he is given Han's medal by Maz Kanata following Leia's death in *The Rise of Skywalker*.

Despite answering her distress call, Obi-Wan Kenobi does not meet Princess Leia in the movie.

Chewbacca was inspired by George Lucas' dog, Indiana.

According to sound designer Ben Burtt, the alien dialogue spoken by the long-nosed creature in Mos Eisley was actually the processed voice of John Wayne.

A small pair of dice can be seen hanging in the *Millennium Falcon* cockpit. Placed there by set decorator Roger Christian, the dice would feature prominently in *The Last Jedi* and *Solo: A Star Wars Story*.

The opening crawl was edited by George Lucas' friend, Brian De Palma.

The full title of the film: *Star Wars: Episode IV A New Hope* first appeared when the film was re-released in 1981.

A New Hope is the only *Star Wars* film, to date, to be nominated in the Best Picture catergory at the Oscars.

The only time we see an Imperial blaster stun someone on the big screen is when Princess Leia is shot at the start of the film.

For the sequel to *Star Wars*, a global smash and a pop cultural phenomenon, George Lucas sent the characters down a darker path, assisted by co-writer Lawrence Kasdan. While the film's battle scenes and scope were bigger than its predecessor, the film tells a more character-led, personal story.

George Lucas (Writer, Executive Producer): *The Empire Strikes Back* is a very different film to the first *Star Wars*. It's rather a sad film—more of a tragedy than a comedy.

Lawrence Kasdan (Writer): George Lucas' grand design for the first three movies was great. The second act of any three-act structure is always the best. You don't have to spend time setting things up and you get to leave the story hanging because you know there is a third act coming—you want everything to be falling apart in the second act. When I started on *Empire*, we were under the gun because the film was in preproduction and they had no script. What George needed was somebody who was going to do what he had in mind. They were highly intense, highly adrenalized, fun sessions with George and the director, Irvin Kershner. I would go away and write, and in two weeks, we'd come back and look at the new draft. I wrote the movie really fast.

Irvin Kershner (Director): I kept thinking in terms of character. George was thinking in terms of actual story and Lawrence Kasdan was thinking of dialogue, which ties the character and story together.

Carrie Fisher (Princess Leia): *The Empire Strikes Back* is much more a film about people. It had more of an ambiance than *Star Wars*. We rehearsed a lot more on *Empire*, but the rewriting and reshooting of

2 /

scenes that didn't work put us over schedule.

Lawrence Kasdan: The main characters were pretty wide open. You can describe characters in one sentence but that doesn't tell you what they are going to say. There were surprises all through the three movies in terms of what the characters' relationships were. George wanted me to write everything and then tell me if he had a problem. He would flip through the pages and not say anything. I finally said, "What's the deal, man?" and he said, "Oh, I forgot to tell you. I won't tell you anything unless I have a problem with it." I said, "Well how about you just tell me when you really love something? I'd

like that!" I made him compliment me occasionally!

George Lucas: I would say that John Williams had the most autonomy since I don't know that much about music. I was able to make some suggestions about what I thought would work and what wouldn't, and found him to be very receptive to making changes. With Kershner, I offered some suggestions, but he was generally on his own to make the film as he saw fit. With the first writer, Leigh Brackett, things were a little different. I gave her a very detailed story and from that she wrote the first draft of the screenplay. Unfortunately, she died soon after the draft was completed. I did several more

1 / Mark Hamill hangs upside down on set as the crew film the sequence in the wampa cave. (Previous spread)

2 / George Lucas and Irvin Kershner interrupt Darth Vader's meditation for a photo opportunity.

3 / The *Millennium Falcon* evades the Empire.

drafts before we found another screenwriter, Lawrence Kasdan. His job was to clean up the script and put on the finishing touches.

Harrison Ford (Han Solo):
The first one was a cakewalk compared to the second one. The second one was more difficult. The relationships became more significant, and the points that needed to be brought across become more subtle. For the first film, a great deal of energy was expended to establish a context for a relatively small story that was heavily plotted and really articulately contrived. The second time, all that is done for you. You can pretty much think that everyone who has seen the second one, has seen the first one. You can just walk on and start the story. I felt a sense of responsibility for making this film better than the first. If you can't do it better, it's boring.

Anthony Daniels (C-3PO):
People knew they were back on some sort of winner with *The Empire Strikes Back*. You only had to look at the script to see that it was very, very good. Most times watching a scene in the studio is very dull. But there were some scenes where people were actually crowding in to watch. There was definitely an air of excitement about this project.

For this film, Lucas elected to hand the directorial reigns over to veteran director, Irvin Kershner.

George Lucas: I've never really enjoyed directing. So [at that point] I more or less retired from directing. I felt that if I directed *Empire*, I'd have to direct the next one, and the one after that, and so on for the rest of my life. Being an executive producer is a much easier job than directing. I generally oversee the production and, although I have less control over specific things, I find I can live a much saner life than as a director!

3 /

4 /

Harrison Ford: The difference in directors was no problem at all. Each director brought different qualities to the same circumstances. George worked more simply, as was appropriate under the circumstances. I think it was a more agonizing task for Kershner. Because of the success of the first one, the responsibilities encumbered in making the second one were far greater. I think he did a good job.

Irvin Kershner: I was thrown into it. I knew nothing of special effects. George had faith in me, and I wanted to prove to him that he was right. I knew George and we played tennis occasionally but when he asked me to do it, I was surprised and frightened. I turned it down at first. I felt to follow *Star Wars* would be to make a film not as good because it would not have the freshness of the original. George explained something to me. He said, "If it isn't as good or better than *Star Wars* then it won't be a series. It'll die right there. It's got to stand up to the original and go beyond it if possible."

Usually, you start a film and the style emerges. However, for *Empire*, I had to make stylistic choices in preproduction. Because of the many scenes that included special effects, it was difficult to move the camera. Therefore, to keep the film from being stiff and static, I had to carefully stage the movement within the frame and keep the camera in movement when there were no special effects. Also, whenever possible, I used action cuts, going from a movement in one scene to a parallel action in the next shot to further create the perception of movement.

Filming commenced in Finse, Norway for the scenes on the remote ice world of Hoth.

Anthony Daniels: The first film shot for fifteen weeks, while this one shot for eighteen weeks, part of that time in Norway. They

5 /

didn't take me to Norway because the C-3PO costume would literally freeze up in that kind of cold.

Harrison Ford: Norway was cold and slow. I hadn't anticipated being there at all. My snow scenes were supposed to be shot on the soundstage at the studio. I had just arrived in England as the cast and crew left for Norway and found myself whisked away to join them with no preparation and wearing a costume built for conditions on the stage. It wasn't as bad for the actors as it was for the crew though. That British crew were incredibly tough. Our shelter was in the back of snowmobiles and such, and we were never able to reach the base camp, which they'd established on a glacier because of the weather.

4 / Filming the opening scene for the film on location in Finse.

5 / Luke (Mark Hamill) and his tauntaun encounter one of the more unfriendly inhabitants of Hoth.

6 / Hamill, Carrie Fisher, and Harrison Ford keep warm on location in Norway.

Peter Mayhew (Chewbacca): I'm most proud of the scene where we're on Hoth and they close the doors and Chewie is standing underneath the *Falcon* holding the ladder and he hears the clanging of the doors. It's the realization that people are still out there and he yells. That's one moment where you see the sympathetic side of Chewie.

Although Kershner was inexperienced with dealing with special effects, George Lucas was able to offer valuable advice.

Irvin Kershner: Before I started, George said, "Remember, nothing is going to work." He meant the special effects on the set and he was right. He also said, "Don't ▶

▶ worry about the special effects. You dream up what you want to do and no matter what they say on set—they'll say that it is impossible—you do it. We'll find a way to make it work." And they always found a way to make it work.

The first shot of the whole film didn't work. We were in Norway and the tauntaun froze up! We couldn't get the smoke to come out of its nose and the movements weren't right because the wiring had frozen. The temperature was twenty six below zero.

When we got back to Elstree, on the first day of shooting, we were in the tunnels of Hoth and R2-D2 was supposed to race along the corridor. Everything was tested the night before; we staged it and lit it. I called "Action!" and he went two feet, started spinning in little circles and didn't go forward. I thought we might never finish the film at this rate! The special effects people fixed it and we started again, and it did the same thing! It worked on floorboards the night before, but they had put artificial ice, which was made from plastic on the floor and R2-D2 didn't work on plastic! I asked them to bring an empty

R2-D2 prop and we put a wire on it and pulled it along. We got that shot in one take!

Phil Tippett (Industrial Light & Magic animation unit): I sculpted a mock-up of the tauntaun and sent it to the *Star Wars* art department in England. There they constructed the full-size, eight-foot-tall model that was used for the close-ups filmed in Norway and at EMI-Elstree Studios. In the meantime, I perfected a twelve-inch tauntaun model to use for the animation. This version was sculpted in clay and then cast into a very flexible rubber material. We built a steel ball and socket skeleton that was put on the inside of the rubber model.

Dennis Muren (miniature and optical effects unit): *The Empire Strikes Back* was the hardest film that I ever worked on, and one of the most rewarding. I thought the work came out really good and I liked the film a lot. That's because we had just moved up from Los Angeles to San Francisco and we had to crew up all the people here, an awful lot of them locally, because we didn't have very many who came up from L.A. for the

show, and it was just very difficult. If you look at *Empire* compared to the original *Star Wars*, it's far more complicated.

John Morton (Dak): The snow that was used was also used in Stanley Kubrick's *The Shining* (1980). It was a substance called dendritic salt that would vaporize a bit. We all had headaches for a while. But everyone had a wonderful time. It was like Christmas; George Lucas set the tone.

Filming conditions did not much improve when Kershner turned his attention to filming scenes of the swampy world of Dagobah.

Irvin Kershner: George visited the set when we were shooting the X-wing being pulled out of the water. It had taken a long time to set up the shot and the haze was right because we closed the set off so that we actually had clouds hanging. The ship looked beautiful with moss and seaweed hanging off it, and suddenly the two wings just collapsed. I felt so badly for George because I knew it was his money. They crew said they hadn't realized it wasn't

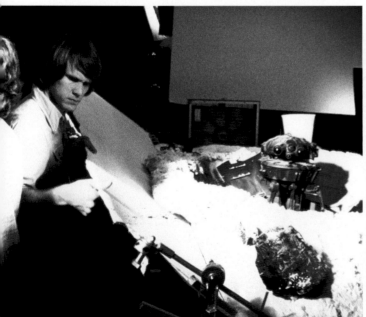

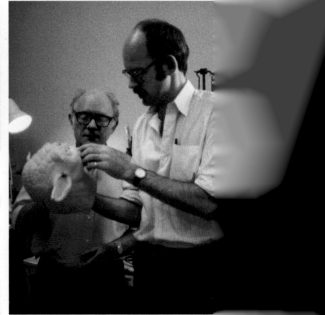

7 /   8 /

waterproof. The wings were made of wood and they couldn't take all the weight. It was rebuilt with steel. It took ten hours to get a six-second shot.

The Empire Strikes Back featured the debut of a new character, who would become one of the best-loved characters of the entire saga, the Jedi Master, Yoda.

Frank Oz (Yoda): Jim Henson was originally asked to perform Yoda but he recommended me because he had a company to run. Gary Kurtz visited me while I was filming *The Muppet Movie* (1979) and showed me a picture of Yoda. Sometimes I have trouble getting

characters, sometimes characters evolve, but Yoda hit immediately off the page for me. I just liked the character and I couldn't actually describe why. That, along with George and Lawrence Kasdan's words were how he came about. What I liked about him was this extraordinarily wise and powerful figure being this little, petty guy. Irvin Kershner suggested the scene where Yoda is fighting with Artoo with his cane. Yoda is like a wise Zen master, but like any Zen master, he'll smack you if you're wrong! I always likened Yoda to Winston Churchill who might be having to make great decisions about the war and yet he's also wondering if he

should take that last candy in the dish or not because he wants it really bad. It's that paradox that makes him more human. Also, so much of why Yoda is successful is because Mark Hamill believed in him. If Mark hadn't responded to Yoda so well, then the audience wouldn't have.

Irvin Kershner: Stuart Freeborn who made Yoda was the sweetest man in the world. He engineered and built Yoda. He did a beautiful job—except when we went to shoot, I couldn't get Yoda to blink! I think I only got two blinks out of him in the whole picture!
    Mark couldn't hear Yoda talk—everyone was under the ▶

7 / Art director Joe Johnston prepares the miniature probe droid for filming.

8 / Frank Oz and Jim Henson take a look at Stuart Freeborn's Yoda head.

9 / Mark Hamill ready for action as he films scenes for the Battle of Hoth.

floorboards. I'm the only one who could hear both of them. We would rehearse and then do a take when we had the timing right. Mark really did a terrific job.

While the movie's twists were kept secret from the cast and crew, an exception was made for a certain Jedi Master.

Frank Oz: They just gave me my scenes and I said, "I can't do this. If I play a character who is the wisest character in the movie, I have to know what is going on in the world he's involved in." I was then sent the full script.

In addition to Yoda, Dagobah's swamps also held other, less friendly inhabitants.

Mark Hamill: I don't mind the snakes that much. I just don't like to handle them. You're cautious with snakes just like you are cautious with any animal. I was all right until one bit me. I was pulling snakes from the X-wing's engines. The handler told me to hold them about eighteen inches from the head so the snake could writhe and everybody could see that it's not rubber. The first one had secreted this milky liquid, which had blinded him. Every time I touched him he flinched, so I flinched. It's some of the best acting I've ever done. I looked so calm and yet inside I was scared! The snake bit me on the eighth take. He wasn't poisonous, but being bitten was scary. The whole film is constructed to make me look like a hero, and I was running around yelling that the snake had bitten me!

The focus on visual effects led to some actors wanting to make sure they had their director's eye.

Irvin Kershner: We were shooting a difficult scene with Harrison and there were some special effects in the scene. We shot it in one take and I said,

"That's it, let's move on" and Harrison stopped. He said, "Wait, was I good or did the special effects work and therefore you don't want to shoot it again?" I said, "Harrison, by now you have to trust me. You were great. The special effects happened to work but you were great." And he looked at me with that wonderful look of his and said, "Uh huh. Okay." And he pointed a finger at me, wagging it and said, "Now, you better watch yourself!"

The film played against audience expectations, not least by splitting up the droids as they embarked on separate adventures.

Anthony Daniels: They gave me Harrison Ford instead of R2-D2. Han Solo was a pretty good R2 substitute. It was a good dramatic coupling. His spikey approach with See-Threepio's need for everything to be proper worked really well.

Mark Hamill: It was wonderful the way they split up the droids, which is the last thing you would

10 / Luke encounters Jedi Master Yoda on the swamp world of Dagobah.

11 / Luke's retrieved X-wing fighter, a scene that proved tough to film.

12 / Stuart Freeborn sculpting the Yoda puppet.

11 /

expect. It was like taking Laurel away from Hardy, but that is the beauty of George's approach— just when you think you know what is coming next, you find out you're wrong!

Anthony Daniels: C-3PO is transparent. I think that is why he is liked by so many people, There's no guile, no deviousness, no mystery. He is so obvious, and he always states the obvious. In the wrong circumstances, that can be very irritating, but it can also be very funny too.

I must be impossible to work with because it is very hard to hear what I say and you can't see my eyes. I bump into my co-stars, I hurt them, jab them with my elbows, and I clank. It can't be much fun!

Striking back as the *Empire*'s finest officers, were two British actors who lent a touch of paranoid menace as they served under the command of Darth Vader.

Kenneth Colley (Admiral Piett): At the time, the most influential American critic was Pauline Kael and she called it the most beautiful -looking film of the year and I think she was spot on. It was shot and framed wonderfully.

Irvin Kershner was great at foreshortening [dialogue]. Irvin was brilliant at just honing it down to a single sentence that did the job. He's a great photographer —he is a great stills photographer of international note anyway, he has exhibitions around the world. That's why it looks so good."

Julian Glover (General Veers): Kenneth Colley and I only filmed for a week. There was one scene with Darth Vader and myself. We didn't meet the main actors. As far as we were concerned, we had no idea of the huge success of *Empire*. At that time, my next-door neighbor was the associate producer Robert Watts and he invited me in. Despite having such ▶

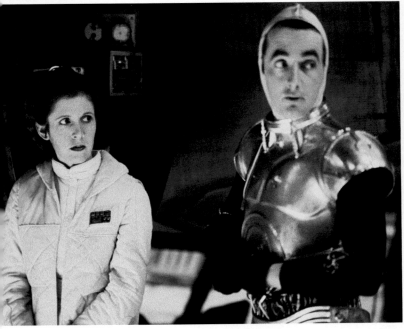

13 /

14 /

13 / Carrie Fisher and Anthony Daniels take a break from shooting.

14 / Darth Vader assembles the bounty hunters in a bid to track down the *Millennium Falcon*.

15 / Irvin Kershner takes a moment to pose with some of the stars of his movie.

16 / Visual effects photographer Ken Ralston photographs Boba Fett's starship.

a small part in it, I think *Empire* is still the best of the lot.

I said to George Lucas "This man is a general. You don't get to be a general if you're a wimp." Of course, you have to be subservient to Darth Vader, he's the guv'nor, but you don't have to be sycophantic. Then [Lucas] said "No, absolutely not." And in that one scene, I stood up to Darth Vader a little.

The film introduced a group of characters, the bounty hunters who would prove hugely popular with fans, including the mysterious Boba Fett.

Jeremy Bulloch (Boba Fett): My half-brother, Robert Watts, said come and see if I fit into the suit. They were looking for people to fit the costume. My whole kit was fairly light. The costume was hot, but I put up with it. Peter Mayhew suffered more than anybody. He must have lost pounds every day.

George Lucas explained that Boba Fett was methodical in his movement. The costume helped a great deal. I think the secret to playing Boba is the less you do, the stronger the character is. There is no point in him waving his gun around. He is very cool. He doesn't move much. I thought of him as Clint Eastwood in armor. He has respect from people because he captured Han Solo. He answers Darth Vader back and he has a fantastic costume.

Alan Harris (Bossk): The gas jet on Boba Fett's wrist was practical, originally—the effects guys made it a working flamethrower but George Lucas decided it was too dangerous. Also, it was bloody heavy!

Jason Wingreen (original voice of Boba Fett): I believe I got the role of Boba Fett's voice because I was up for the voice of Yoda prior to Frank Oz being cast. I also ended up doing the voiceover for *The Empire Strikes Back* underwear line!

John Morton: Steve Lanning, the second assistant director, and Jeremy Bulloch asked me to cover as Boba Fett for a couple of days so I played him in the scene where he confronts Vader and says, "He's no good to me dead."

Irvin Kershner: Boba Fett is memorable. The name is a good one; George has a way with names. I don't know where he gets them from. We made Boba Fett look like he's been through hell. He is a frightening dramatic element to create tension that puts Han Solo in danger. I guess the look was okay because the dolls have sold!

The Empire Strikes Back featured the debut of Lando Calrissian, the Baron Administrator of Cloud City as played by the suave and debonair actor, Billy Dee Williams. Calrissian is assisted by Lobot, his aide.

Billy Dee Williams (Lando Calrissian): Lando is a guy who belongs in the future. He has transcended all the questions and dilemmas that we face, the usual antiquated ideas about what a person is and what a person should be. I had a good intelligent understanding of the character. I really wanted to make him a dashing guy.

Being a hero was a big part of my thinking at the time

because I really wanted to create something that nobody seemed to want to look at. I have always seen myself that way and I wanted to present myself that way. So it worked.

I tried to make Lando a romantic character but there is also an absurdity to him. I see myself as a walking absurdity.

John Hollis (Lobot): If you've got a part where you are walking around with lights flashing on your head, you can't really fail, can you? Originally, Lobot had quite a few lines but they were just questions put to him by Lando so I wasn't too bothered to see them go. The headpiece

15 /

was murder to wear. It had to be self-contained, so it was battery powered and very heavy. I was glad to take it off at the end of the day.

Lando's dubious allegiances in the movie led to Williams having to answer some tough questions from younger fans.

Billy Dee Williams: When the movie came out, I would pick my daughter up from school and these kids would run up to me and say, "You betrayed Han Solo!" I would find myself trying to explain the whole situation! Lando loses everything. He even stands up to Darth Vader, which most people don't do.

Further challenges were presented when filming a pivotal scene on the uncomfortable carbon freezing chamber set.

Jeremy Bulloch: There was steam coming up from the floor. It was so hot that David Prowse and I had to have our helmets taken off every three minutes. We were dripping with sweat. I remember treading on his cape coming down the stairs of the carbon freezing chamber. I trod on an Ugnaught and there was a yelp. I thought it was a real Ugnaught noise!

Irvin Kershner used to shout out directions for that particular scene. And then ask, "Have you said your lines Boba?" because no one could hear what I was saying under the helmet.

Carrie Fisher: The most trouble we had was when the scene is written by, for instance, Harrison and the director, without my being there. The scene where Harrison said, "I know" was rewritten and was great, but I just felt that I needed to be present when a scene that concerns me is redone. We didn't have any trouble doing that scene because Harrison and I know each other

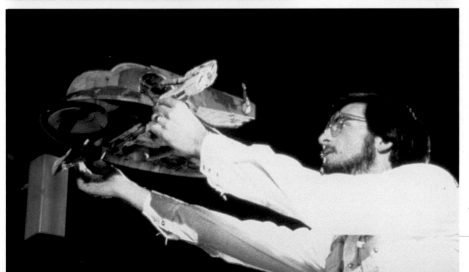

16 /

▶

17 /

> " Darth Vader saying
> 'I am your father' made
> perfect sense for this movie. "
>
> Lawrence Kasdan

▶ so well. After all the publicity tours and talking about ourselves and the movies endlessly, we developed ways of getting through scenes like that.

Alan Harris (Bossk): Originally, they made a complete body mold around me for Harrison Ford, but they decided they wanted something people could carry, so they made another one on the floor. Harrison's head was added to the prop to give the illusion he was frozen in carbonite.

Anthony Daniels: It was a disgusting set because it was so steamy, and there was a horrible smell of wet rust in the air. It was actually not very pleasant. I was on Chewbacca's back. There was fog or incense added for atmosphere.

Peter Mayhew: See-Threepio was in a cargo net, and the net was attached to my back, and underneath the costume, there was a body belt, and the top half of Threepio's body was literally hung from a bucket. His arms were tied with fishing line, which ran under the costume and onto my hands, so as I ran, his hands moved in the opposite direction! The head was moved by having a thin line down though the neck under my shoulder onto the finger of my hand, so as I moved my hands, his head swiveled! It weighed thirty or forty pounds. Those four days of shooting were the worst.

Mayhew, clad in hot fur and carrying more than most, had additional difficulties filming on the Cloud City set.

Peter Mayhew: One Friday afternoon, we were filming on Cloud City. We were doing all the chases through the corridors out to where the *Falcon* was docked and I took a hard right down the corridor while lugging fifty pounds worth of Threepio on my back and everything just went black. The next thing I knew, I was on the ground and everybody was crowded around me. They checked that I was breathing and assumed that I was all right. They were more worried about any damage to Threepio!

They decided to try a body double to give me a break and it didn't work at all. The guy wasn't as tall as I was, and didn't have double joints, so there's no way that somebody could imitate how I played the character. That information was inside my head —you couldn't put it down on paper. We re-shot the scenes again on Monday and it was all OK.

The film climaxed with a major revelation that changed the shape of the saga.

Mark Hamill: Luke failed when he went to Bespin. Some feel it was earlier, when Luke took his lightsaber into the cave, despite Yoda's warning. Yoda was telling Luke that in the larger scope of things, weapons were not important. In a conflict of the human element, like between father and son, your priorities have to be very clear. Luke's failure was in leaving Dagobah much too early. The confrontation on Bespin was pretty much one-sided. Luke was proficient as a swordsman but suddenly realized that Vader had only drawn him to Cloud City to lure him to the dark side.

Lawrence Kasdan: Darth Vader saying, "I am your father" made perfect sense for the movie. Most movies are about the same issue— about how part of you wants to follow your desires and the other part wants to do what's right. One is the dark side and the other is the light side. We all face this every day. That's what most art is about.

James Earl Jones (Voice of Darth Vader): Darth Vader doesn't express himself with his voice. The words are there, he just lays it out and that's it. Vader is a man who never learned about the ▶

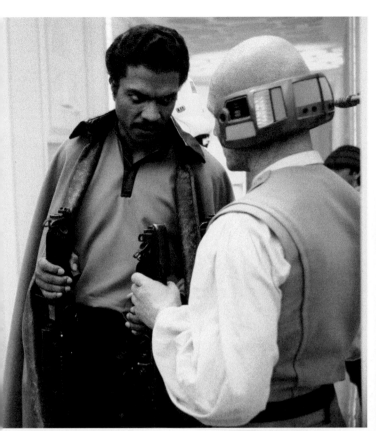

beauties and subtilties of human expression. We figured the key to my work was to keep it on a very narrow band of expression. There was no way to enlighten that voice with an awareness. I had to keep the awareness out of Darth Vader's voice—take all humanity out of it. It was also important that he not sound like an American and to keep it universal, like he could be from anywhere, anytime.

I recall thinking that Vader was lying when he said, "I am your father." At the time, I just didn't know for sure. It deepened who Darth Vader was. I didn't question anything. I just read the lines.

Irvin Kershner: One of the most difficult things was shooting Darth Vader talking to Luke who's hanging thirty feet above the ground, held up by a little wire. Two giant fans were blowing him, and he was shouting out lines that had nothing to do with what everybody else heard, because the crew didn't know about Vader being Luke's father. David Prowse, who was playing Vader, didn't know either! I gave him lines so that his actions would match what he seemed to be saying. Nobody could hear the lines except me and Mark. Mark's emotions were perfect.

Despite the difficulties during the production, the cast did find time to have fun on set.

Kenny Baker (R2-D2): My two boys would come on set and play in the cockpit of the *Falcon* with Peter Mayhew, Harrison Ford, and Mark Hamill in-between takes. My youngest son Kevin, who was four at the time, didn't have his two front teeth and just couldn't say "Harrison." One day Harrison said, "Listen kid, if you can't say Harrison, just call me Peaches," at which point Mark Hamill came over and said, "Well if you're calling him Peaches, you'd better call me Cream!"

Denis Lawson (Wedge Antilles): For some reason, Wedge was alive at the end of *Star Wars*. When I saw the film for the first time at the cast and crew screening, I thought that my character had been blown up! And then I got the call for the sequel. I had time to do the second film and had become friends with Mark Hamill. When we made the second one, our wives were both pregnant. Mark used to reference me as George Lucas' Token Survivor!

Billy Dee Williams: It was difficult at first because I was the new boy on the block. They were like a little family—and that's what George creates; he creates a family.

Irvin Kershner: Working on *Empire* was a very good experience, despite its complexity and difficulties. I always felt that there was a caring organization backing me up, supervised by George Lucas, that understood filmmaking. Usually there's a lot of ego involved but there was none with *Empire*. Even though it took over two and half years to make, it was one of the best experiences I've ever had.

22 /

21 / Carrie Fisher and Harrison Ford share a light moment on set.

22 / Gary Kurtz, George Lucas, and Irvin Kershner try to overcome the challenges of filming on the Dagobah set.

23 / Mark Hamill films on the Cloud City set.

Mark Hamill: *Empire* reminds me of a time in our lives when we leave home and discover it can be a hard world out there. I was surprised and delighted over *Empire*'s success even more than *Star Wars*. *Star Wars* became a pop phenomenon so you really can't judge its success and *Empire*'s with the same box office yardstick. It was the profits from *Empire*, not *Star Wars,* that made possible the rest of the *Star Wars* movies that George Lucas had already planned. ☺

STAR WARS: THE EMPIRE STRIKES BACK

ESSENTIAL TRIVIA

The scene in which the rebel characters visit Luke as he recovers from the wounds inflicted by the wampa is the only scene in the movie where Luke, Han, and Leia are all together.

The Empire Strikes Back is the only movie in the first six *Star Wars* films not to have scenes on Tatooine. However, Luke's homeworld does get a mention at the end.

The 1979 trailer for the film was narrated by Harrison Ford.

The actor Treat Williams plays an unnamed rebel in Echo Base, while *Star Wars* concept artist Ralph McQuarrie appears in a fleeting cameo.

According to sound designer Ben Burtt, the sound of the Imperial probe droid is the voice of a well-known Shakespearean actor changed electronically.

Han Solo is the only non-Jedi character to use a lightsaber in the original trilogy.

The Empire Strikes Back was the first *Star Wars* movie to have an episode designation on its initial release.

Lando Calrissian was originally named Lando Kadar, and he was a clone.

Darth Vader's meeting with the Emperor was changed in the 2004 DVD release to feature Ian McDiarmid as the villain.

Among the asteroids, the ILM team added a tennis shoe and a potato. They are near impossible to spot.

Mark Hamill voiced the announcement, "The first transport is away!" during the evacuation of Echo Base.

For the 1997 Special Edition, Luke's dialogue to R2-D2, "You're lucky you don't taste good," was altered to, "You're lucky you got out of there."

Though TIE fighters are featured prominantly, we never see a close-up of a TIE fighter pilot in the cockpit in this film.

Contrary to popular opinion, the wampa attack was not written to explain the scars incurred by Mark Hamill's car accident.

Han's rescue of Luke on the frozen wastes of Hoth was shot by a somewhat comfortable crew. They were positioned in the doorway of their hotel so the camera wouldn't freeze; the actors worked outdoors in sub-freezing temperatures!

The interior of the space slug was created by placing black plastic on the floor of the Echo Base hangar set and draping black curtains around the *Millennium Falcon*. Dry ice was released to complete the effect.

Actress Carrie Fisher was a foot shorter than Harrison Ford. As a result, some of their scenes together had to be filmed with her perched on a box.

During the London stage of shooting, Carrie Fisher rented a house belonging to Monty Python star, Eric Idle.

Filming on *Empire* was delayed because of a fire on the set of Stanley Kubrick's horror film, *The Shining* (1980).

Mark Hamill, Anthony Daniels, and Peter Mayhew appeared on *The Muppet Show* (1976-1981) to promote the release of the movie.

The distinctive groan of the tauntaun was provided by a sea otter named Moda.

The Empire Strikes Back has the lowest body-count of the saga. It's also the only *Star Wars* film in which no major characters die.

The carbon-freeze chamber scene is the only time Darth Vader and C-3PO are in the same room in the original trilogy.

On the day Mark Hamill was filming on the weather vane beneath Cloud City, he received news that his wife had given birth to their first child, Nathan.

Some of the vines used to dress the Dagobah set were used on the temple set during the opening scenes of *Raiders of the Lost Ark* (1981).

The customary reference to George Lucas' classic 1971 movie *THX 1138* occurs early in the film, when General Rieekan says, "Send Rogues ten and eleven to station three-eight."

STAR WARS

RETURN OF THE JEDI

The final chapter of the original trilogy, *Return of the Jedi* marked the end for many plot threads that had been established in *A New Hope*, bringing to a close the story of Darth Vader. For this entry in the saga, director Richard Marquand took audiences to the heart of the criminal underworld on Tatooine, the lush Forest Moon of Endor, and up close to the Emperor himself as Luke Skywalker fought to redeem his father.

Mark Hamill (Luke Skywalker): What makes *Return of the Jedi* great is the four hours of what was the most elaborate set up in the history of filmmaking. This was the last of the trilogy, so there was no reason for us to save anything. We reached the pinnacle of the rollercoaster. It's a white knuckler, straight down from here!

Lawrence Kasdan (Co-writer): I wasn't really writing anymore at this stage, but George had been really helpful to me and asked for a favor. Richard Marquand and George had intense meetings. He had written a previous draft and we did it really quickly and nailed it down. *Return of the Jedi* was a much tougher movie than *The Empire Strikes Back* to pull off because everything has to work out in the end.

Carrie Fisher (Princess Leia): Leia's character undergoes quite a change in *Return of the Jedi*. They found a way for her to be very nice while remaining strong and committed. At least I wasn't always telling Harrison what to do.

Mark Hamill: Luke's character undergoes a natural progression from farm boy to contender to champ. This is the central theme of the adventures of Luke Skywalker. Luke had a lot of anger in him in *Empire*. In *Jedi*, he has grown up. He develops an Obi-Wan-like inner strength.

I don't like to play the same character over and over again but Luke changes so much that I'm never repeating myself.

Richard Marquand (Director): I think any successful drama contains an enormous amount of myth. Otherwise, what is it? It's superficial or of no significance. My previous experience with this aspect of drama has to do with working as a theater director with the Jacobean plays of Marlowe or Shakespeare. These men were the great mythmakers of their time.

The *Star Wars* saga seems to invite comparison to other tales

1 / Luke Skywalker and Darth Vader (Mark Hamill and David Prowse) pose for a family photo. (Previous spread)

2 / Harrison Ford and George Lucas in discussion in the Redwood forest.

3 / George Lucas calls "action" to a startled Richard Marquand, who had a cameo role in the film as an AT-ST driver.

4 / George Lucas looks over designs for the Emperor with costume designer Aggie Rodgers, director Richard Marquand, and costume designer Nilo Rodis-Jamero.

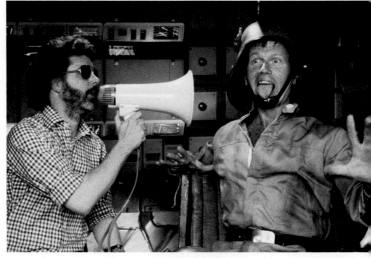

3 /

and myths, but the fact is that it is a true saga completely on its own terms. Kids in Hong Kong and Peru don't know the story of Robin Hood or King Arthur. What they talk about is Luke Skywalker. The strong mythological quality is why, although they don't quite realize it, people go back to the *Star Wars* saga time and time again.

In the early stages, I was so amazed that anybody would consider me as the director of such a rich film, that I almost balked at it. I thought that there must be an older, wiser director with more experience who would be the right person to do this. But George convinced me that I was the right person. As it turned out, I was extremely comfortable. And it was, in fact, a remarkable experience. I didn't know, going in, that it would be such fun. Also, I don't think I ever worked so hard.

4 /

▶ Luke Skywalker was given a new look for this movie, with the actor making suggestions to George Lucas.

Mark Hamill: George was very amiable as far as suggestions go. I found a photograph of a character in a book about Akira Kurosawa, with shaved widow's peaks and a top knot with a bone in it, and an eagle's claw earing. I decided that was Luke's new look! When I brought that photo to George, his face remained the same, but his eyes turned into little kaleidoscopes of fear! I thought Luke's hair should have been shorter, more military looking but George was worried that with the black costume, it might come off a little stiff and stark. I told George that my costume was very Vaderish and he said, "It's supposed to be."

Filming commenced with a sequence that ended up being omitted from the final cut.

Richard Marquand: A director often asks, "What is the very worst thing we could make the heroes do?" So, we invented a sandstorm which we didn't use!

The film opens with the visit to Jabba the Hutt's palace. First mentioned in *A New Hope*, the film would resolve the story of Han Solo's debt to the criminal kingpin and introduce some memorable creatures in doing so.

Anthony Daniels (C-3PO): The set seemed so claustrophobic and dark, which wasn't helped by the incense used to give "atmosphere" —a kind of nightclub fog. For me, Jabba's palace was a trial by smoke! But it looked good, and in a movie, that's what counts.

For the most part, the space was rather crowded with rubber-headed creatures, but the crew squeezed in too. Carrie [Fisher] felt a lot better after she took off her Boushh mask. A role

like C-3PO would not be an option for Carrie! But then, I wouldn't relish sitting around in her metal truss either. I think she felt a bit conspicuous on the first day. But on a set, you get used to odd experiences very quickly. Or you get another job.

Toby Philpott (Jabba the Hutt, puppeteer): After the period of fittings, and a brief practice, we found ourselves arriving onto a very busy set, and climbing inside Jabba through a hole underneath. From then on, Dave [Barclay] and I were mainly alone apart from when Mike Edmonds was in there, too, whenever the tail was in the shot! We had headsets, so we could talk to the rest of the team (operating the eyes by radio control, and so on). We could also hear Richard Marquand's instructions. Dave did the right arm and operated the mouth, and spoke for Jabba, delivering the lines in English for the actors. We always worked Jabba as a unified being, an actor, which meant we were continuously practicing our coordination. Apart from tea breaks and lunch, we stayed inside all day (from 8:30am to 6:00pm).

Richard Marquand: As a director, you are talking to Jabba himself. You're telling him what to do. In the early stages, when you are casting the people who will later play the characters, you are thinking of them as manipulators. At that point, you are interested in their shape or personality and temperament— whether they can stand being in costume for any length of time. But once they are on set and they are in costume, they are that character—I definitely deal with Jabba on set.

Anthony Daniels: I absolutely *loved* Jabba! I'd seen him grow up from a maquette in the Creature Shop, to a wire frame, to a great glob of clay,

5 /

transformed into this jolly green slug. I thought he was great fun on the outside! Inside was a gang of performers who made me laugh all the time. Mike Edmonds starred as the tail, thrashing about. Jabba's right hand, Dave [Barclay] and I had wireless communication so we could hear each other's lines. We used it mainly to gossip and discuss Carrie Fisher's near-costume! Then there was the gang on the outside, remotely controlling Jabba's eyes in an effect that I'd never seen before, focusing and narrowing, just like the eyes of a real Hutt. The other delight of working with Jabba was that he didn't wander off the set or have a bad hair day or a bad makeup moment. So lots of time hanging around in the gold suit was saved there! ▶

5 / Luke threatens Jabba the Hutt during a tense moment in the gangster's palace.

6 / Mark Hamill tries out his new costume as George Lucas looks on.

▶ **Tim Rose (Salacious B. Crumb, Sy Snootles):** The cantina scene in the first film had always made a big impression on people, and we wanted to make our scene as good as that one. There was a good week's worth of lead-time on the scene, and all the characters that we had built in Phil Tippett's shop at Industrial Light & Magic needed to get unpacked and assigned to performers to rehearse with. I already knew several of the performers, because we had worked together on *The Dark Crystal* (1982) for Jim Henson. I was happy with the way Salacious Crumb was coming along, but Sy Snootles was a different matter. I had designed her as a "reverse-string marionette," which was a term I made up. Instead of being controlled by strings from above, as a classic marionette would be, she floated in the air and was pulled down to the ground by wires and rods to the bottoms of her feet. She was very hard to control, and I could only get a good take about once every twelve attempts. When it came time to shoot, they only gave me two takes to get it right, neither of which was one of my good ones. I think that's probably why she got replaced by CGI so early on.

The dark, steamy set proved difficult to shoot on and led to some mishaps along the way.

Toby Philpott: All we could see was a grainy "security camera" shot of Jabba on tiny monitors hanging on our chests, which made filming hard. Dave told me he had to put his hand (Jabba's right hand) on Leia's shoulder, but heard Carrie say (quite calmly) "That's not my shoulder…"

I had to menace Leia with the tongue—my right hand was inside the tongue. We did a couple of takes. Then I heard Mr. Marquand in my headset, asking me to try to reach the tongue farther out, and really try to lick her. On the next take I did just that, but heard a

7 /

stifled gasp, and some laughter, and "CUT!" Only much later was I told I had stuck that horrible, gloop-covered tongue right in Carrie Fisher's ear!

Carrie Fisher: I was not actually a damsel in distress, I was a distressing damsel!

Tim Rose: Salacious spent a lot of time sitting near Jabba's tail. Mike Edmonds was inside the body of Jabba and was controlling his tail with a cable-control mechanism. When he would get bored between takes, he would start swinging the tail back and forth shouting, "Batter up!" and try to knock Salacious off my arm, which he managed to do on more than one occasion!

Anthony Daniels: My bad moment, apart from smelling like a BBQ every evening, was the *great fall*. Jabba was unhappy with Threepio not being helpful enough (as if!) and swiped him with his mighty fist! This meant that I had to fall down. It's easy enough to do by accident in the desert, or in Padmé's apartment, but deliberately? In that costume? To the ground? Not so much.

As an unnamed crewmember was about to leave the set, they asked him to hold the other side of a padded board on which I would fall, just clearing frame. "Action!" Jabba gave me a smack (sort of) and I spun and fell. "Cut!" Good. Now there was blood. I checked. Not mine. But that unnamed crewmember had taken a blow

7 / The droids join Jabba as they go in front of the cameras.

8 / Salacious B. Crumb poses with Carrie Fisher.

9 / Bib Fortuna welcomes another bounty hunter to Jabba's palace.

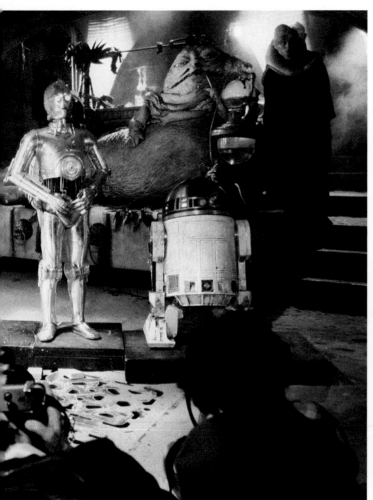

9 /

from Threepio's elbow and was henceforth known as "Scarchin!"

Then, of course, I could tell the dreadful truth about Jabba's slime, but that's another story!

Michael Carter (Bib Fortuna): I liked Bib. He was stupid in an endearing way—quite innocent yet quite scary. The makeup had a feminine look. The makeup dictates your performance. The first time I put it on, it took eight and a half hours. Eventually, Nick Dudman, the makeup artist, got it down to fifty-nine minutes. Once the headpiece was on, it was on all day. One day, I had a terrible itch and after six hours, I was ready to give my children away! Nick split it open down the middle and I scratched. From then on, he made

the headpiece able to open up in the middle.

It was tremendous fun. All the creatures would come by my dressing room. You'd walk in, and there'd be four or five creatures having a coffee!

In a first for the saga, an elaborate song-and-dance number featured Oola, an ill-fated dancing girl who fell foul of Jabba's anger.

Femi Taylor (Oola): We worked on the choreography for two weeks, but they didn't tell me what I would be wearing. All of a sudden, I have to wear this headpiece. It then became a matter of getting used to it and making it your friend. Jabba the Hutt was pretty disgusting, although the

men operating him on the inside were really lovely!

It was quite tricky to dance, since the leash was around five meters long, and the fact that the puppeteers couldn't see me that well, resulted in me being nearly strangled a couple of times! I was fortunate enough to have Mark Hamill come over to introduce himself, and every day he would see if I was okay. And Salacious Crumb was an real irritant, irrespective of Tim Rose being the puppeteer!

Tim Rose: When I sat at the front of Jabba's throne watching some poor soul being fed to the rancor, my body was inside the slab of the throne with my arm up through a hole operating Salacious. I could ▶

▶ only get in though the back of the throne, and that was only when the throne had been pulled back over the stage pit. When it was forward, the exit was blocked. One day, when they called lunch, everybody took off for the canteen and no one remembered to pull the throne back, so I missed lunch that day!

The scenes also marked the return of fan-favorite bounty hunter, Boba Fett, as played by Jeremy Bulloch.

Jeremy Bulloch (Boba Fett): I was literally on the set for about eight days. I always used to get there early, which I have done my whole career, and I'd come out with the helmet in my hand and stand next to Jabba the Hutt, which was like a heap because it wasn't alive. There was Mike Edmonds inside Jabba, moving the tail, and I used to say to Mike, "Get us a cup of tea, will you? I can't move up here." And he used to say, "Get it yourself!" "Mike, you can't see how uncomfortable I am up here." So we'd have this wonderful conversation and every morning Mike would be there ready with a cup of tea! I couldn't stand around too long—I had to lean against a board for comfort.

There were a lot of guys dressed up as aliens, and the set was so good because it was damp; you felt the greasy, oily, nastiness of Jabba all around the place. It was slimy and it had absolutely the right atmosphere. If anybody came in, I would think, *Is he a suitable prey?* and I would move forward very gently. I'd think, *How could Boba Fett do something in this scene to look cool?* You use the time to be as deadly, but as subtle as possible, and with a little bit of fun within it because Boba Fett must never stand out of that circle—he's got to be in charge. He commands without even saying anything.

Richard Marquand's directions were subtle, you just listened to

10 /

what he was saying. He knew where the angles were, how one tilt of the head could get that bit of light glinting off the helmet.

Tim Rose: Richard Marquand used to talk to the Salacious Crumb puppet all the time. When you are doing a good job with a puppet, people treat the puppet as if he is the actor. He found it really funny that this silly little rubber monster could comment on camera angles and things like that.

Many performers took multiple roles, often in the same scenes.

Simon Williamson (Max Rebo, Gamorrean Guard): To have characters and objects to which you can physically relate and touch is so much easier than bluescreen. In one sequence, I was a Gamorrean guard looking down on myself as another Gamorrean guard, falling through the floor and being attacked by the rancor. Then, across the room, there I am as Max Rebo!

My work on *The Dark Crystal* (1982) prepared me for Max Rebo. Although Max is bulky, you needed to be agile and fit to get inside the costume, and then have

10 / The arrival of Boushh and the mighty Chewbacca is captured by the cameras.

11 / Sir Alec Guinness and Mark Hamill film a crucial expository scene. The shimmering Force spirit effect seen around Guinness will be added later by the visual effects team.

the stamina to cope with the heat. Picture the scene—a Gamorrean guard with a cooling fan wedged between my propped-open jaws and a hairdryer thrust down the front of my trousers! It's a lot of fun playing large, lumbering, stupid characters with mucus dribbling out of their noses. I used to get rid of my aggression by doing karate, but as a Gamorrean guard, I rarely had to attack anyone, I just threatened to dribble all over them!

A return to the Dagobah set gave Luke Skywalker the chance to say goodbye to Yoda, and Mark Hamill the chance to say goodbye to Alec Guinness, at least on the *Star Wars* set.

Mark Hamill: I was so lucky to work with someone I admired for so long. He was so gracious with his time. He stayed in contact, corresponding with beautiful calligraphy in old-fashioned ink. I would see him in London, and we'd go out to dinner. He was one of the greatest actors ever.

The Rebel Alliance, introduced a new leader and, for the first time, some new alien allies.

Caroline Blakiston (Mon Mothma): Mon Mothma is calm, and she looks in charge. I wasn't calm when I did my scene. I was nervous because I was given all these new lines to learn and I like lines to be inside me for a long time so that I can really re-invent them when I'm speaking, as if I had just thought of them. I timed how long I was on screen. It was twenty-seven and a half seconds! I can remember telling Carrie Fisher, "You're all over my daughter's pyjamas!"

Tim Rose (Admiral Ackbar): Admiral Ackbar was sitting on a stand in the corner of the studio and I said to Phil Tippett [make-up and creature design], "Who is that? Can I play him?" and begged ▶

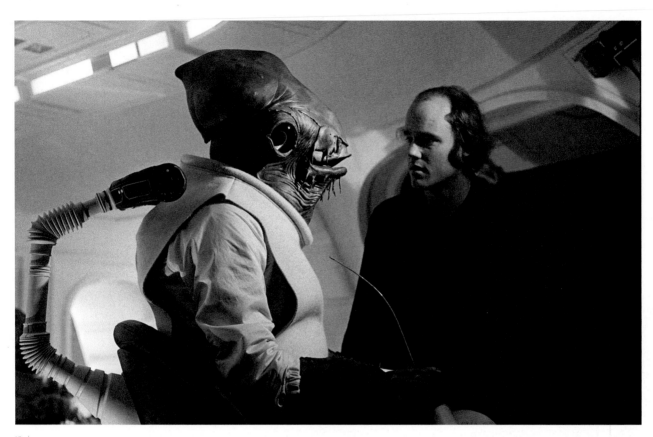

12 /

to play this background character, thinking he was going to be in the third row of Jabba's palace or something. To be honest, I think he ended up commanding the troops—not so much down to my performance but because of his look! He was originally meant to be a background character. He ended up filling the role because he had the magic. There was a character next to him with three eyes who could have been chosen. Ackbar had cables for the eyes, but he was a hand puppet. The mouth was performed remotely when I was walking around in the full body suit. For the close ups, I was the chest of it and operating the head like a puppet.

Ben Burtt (Sound Designer): Nien Nunb spoke Haya, an African dialect from Kenya. We got Kipsang Rotich, a student from Kenya to speak that. We used a lot of Haya phrases, which were recognized when the film played

there! Fortunately, he was saying things that were comprehensible to the story.

Filming in the Redwood Forest, doubling for the Ewok's home of Endor, proved an exotic— and occasionally hazardous —location for the cast and crew.

Warwick Davis (Wicket W. Warrick): Richard Marquand was a very considered director. He wasn't one of those directors who yelled or anything like that. He would quietly talk you through what was happening. I got on with the job at hand and interpreted it in my own way by adding things in, like tilting my head from side to side.

Kenny Baker, who is best known as Artoo-Detoo, and I had a scene together. Kenny (as an Ewok called Paploo) would always jiggle around quite a lot and looked like he was in a hurry. Richard noticed that I'd started

to take on those little traits. He said, "Go and be your own character. You don't have to copy Kenny. Keep doing it in your own style, because that's what we love." Wicket's a lot more chilled out than Paploo.

It's a trap you can fall into as an actor. If someone is doing an accent, you can end up doing the accent as well, if you're not careful. Richard steered me back on course and we carried on from there.

Kenny Baker (R2-D2, Paploo): Someone noticed a huge branch that was sticking across another branch. The trees were 250 feet high. If that branch had been blown down, it would have come down like a spear. So, they brought in two sharpshooters, but the bullets just splintered through the wood. So, we had to move the entire set. They just couldn't risk the branch falling and killing someone.

12 / Phil Tippett and his iconic creation, Admiral Ackbar.

13 / Richard Marquand directs Harrison Ford.

14 / The *Millennium Falcon* on the sound stage used for the ultimately deleted sandstorm sequence.

15 / Sound designer Ben Burtt surrounded by actors inside the Ewok costumes, including a young Warwick Davis (to his left). (Overleaf)

Warwick Davis: Kenny Baker was playing Wicket and I was cast as a background Ewok, but Kenny fell ill on the day of an important scene. George Lucas noticed I was doing interesting things with the character and my costume was cuter than some of the others. And I was the only one who could poke my tongue out of the costume. I ended up filming a scene with Princess Leia and the rest is history!

Ben Burtt: For the Ewoks, we used a lot of Kalmuck, a nomadic tribesman dialect. When you use a real language, there is an intelligence behind it and a reality and detail that is hard to invent.

Kenny Baker: Playing Paploo was not fun at all! If I fell over, I couldn't get up again. I couldn't get in or out of the costume without a dresser. If I fell, I had to wait for someone to rescue me. I had pajamas on then a foam rubber suit and then a fur skin. On top of that there was the belt, armor, headdress, and gloves and feet. The Ewoks were great characters but I don't think I could play one again.

13 /

Warwick Davis: They used to call me the "Ever-Ready Ewok" because I was so young and could keep going in the heat! Every time a shot ended, it was "Heads off!" Our eyes kept misting up.

Anthony Daniels: I was asked to come in on Monday, prepared to mime the story of *A New Hope*, *The Empire Strikes Back*, and up to that point, *Return of the Jedi*. I went home, pushed the sitting room furniture aside and started working on ideas. But rehearsing on the set with Harrison Ford staring sardonically at you while you're saying, "Teekolo carbonite" and "Gooboo Sarlacc" can be a little bit embarrassing!

Warwick Davis: I remember it being very cold; it was a very cold winter when we were shooting in the U.K. We would come out of the soundstage at Elstree. There were two soundstages next to each other; one with the Ewok village set and the other with the *Millennium Falcon*. When you walked between the stages, there was a sheltered area. You'd not get rained on, but the ends were open to the elements, so the wind would blow down. We'd walk down in the Ewok suits, steaming, and a lovely cold draught would blow down this alleyway and keep us cool.

On the set, there were some log cabins where we'd sit and relax while waiting for the next set-up. Back in those days, they'd use incense to give a haze to the atmosphere and the smell was quite overwhelming. If I smell incense now, I can be transported right back to the Ewok village.

Working in those conditions was pretty oppressive. It was hot for the crew, let alone the Ewoks! Then you've got the smoke and the lights, and you're working twenty feet off the ground! It was a difficult environment to be in and there wasn't much room with all the equipment and crew. It was quite a challenge to shoot. ▶

14 /

Anthony Daniels: Nothing for Threepio is easy and that's a good comic setup. He's funny because he has no sense of humor. The nearest he gets is when he says, "I'm rather embarrassed, General Solo, but it appears you are to be the main course at a banquet in my honor." This is said with a certain amount of irony, but Threepio is not a stand-up comic.

Peter Mayhew (Chewbacca): *Star Wars* was all made on sets, *Empire* was often cold and wet and miserable, but *Return of the Jedi* was on terra firma. It was the nicest of the lot. It has some nice comedy, particularly in the Ewok battle scene.

Anthony Daniels: I loved the bit where Han keeps tapping C-3PO on the shoulder and giving him things to do until Threepio just turns and gives Han this look that says, "You insufferable jerk." I was pretty proud of Threepio for that.

The movie also revealed the surprise revelation that Luke and Leia were in fact siblings.

Carrie Fisher: I was *very* surprised. We had different colored eyes! But it meant I got to date Han Solo!

The central story of Luke's confrontation with Darth Vader reached a climax in the third act of the film, and also brought the sinister Emperor into sharp focus.

Richard Marquand: Darth Vader is popular, not just because his is a baddie—although they are usually the most interesting characters— but because of other fascinating things about him. One is that he has a kind of subtle sense of humor, which makes him more attractive than some of the other bad guys. In *Return of the Jedi,* he is only really outflanked by the real bad guy who has an even better sense of humor, as well as being more evil. Vader has a wry, mean way of looking at life

16 /

because he is a wry, mean man. Ultimately, you don't really know who he is. He provokes the same curiosity as the Mona Lisa: *why is she smiling?* You keep coming back to Darth Vader: *who is in there?*

Mark Hamill: It's very hard for the Royal Shakespearian actors playing Imperial guards to act with a barely audible Dave Prowse. He has great presence, but he couldn't be heard in the mask. That's what we are up against. Anytime you work with creatures or in any scenes where there is smoke or when the actors voice is not going to be used in the mix, you are bound to have some trouble. It's the most unnatural form of acting.

Ian McDiarmid (The Emperor): I came into *Return of the Jedi* fairly late in the day. Mary Selway, the casting director, had seen me play many years older than my years in a play called *Seduced*. She recommended me to George and Richard, we had a brief meeting, and before I knew it, I was playing the part! They gave me the tape of the Emperor's appearance in *The Empire Strikes Back* and asked me to match Clive Revill's vocal style. I reckon that's what I would have wanted to use anyway. As things went on, I saw the makeup and saw myself in the mirror and got to know the him a bit better and the voice just came. It's much lower than my own and sharper. I knew it had to be deep and animal-like. But a sophisticated animal. As he gets

16 / Harrison Ford and Mark Hamill take a break on the Ewok village set.

17 / Richard Marquand directs Ian McDiarmid and Mark Hamill as Luke is tempted by the dark side.

18 / Carrie Fisher and Mark Hamill have a laugh on set.

older, when he becomes a bitter and desiccated man, I thought he was like a toad.

George Lucas gave very little, really. I read the books and worked things out, but I think it's quite good that I knew as little as I did. I was left with the best tools, which are just the lines, the other actors, and the situation. He's a mysterious, dark character, and I wouldn't want to do anything to dispel the mystery or lighten the darkness.

Mark Hamill: Learning swordplay is like learning choreography when you do a musical. It's [fight arranger] Peter Diamond's job to make me look good. In *Jedi*, we were much more interested in the personal conflicts involved than lots of flashy swordplay.

Ian McDiarmid: All the readings of the Emperor's lines were my own. I'd discuss it with Richard Marquand and we would suggest things to each other. The lines are very fun and simple. They don't really have any subtext. If you wield that kind of power, you don't have to bother with subtext. You just say and enact what you feel. I enjoyed those scenes because I was working with a very fine actor, Mark Hamill. Mark and I were able to laugh between takes—although when I laughed, it hurt because of the makeup!

Richard Marquand: The temptations facing Luke are so enormous that you could not see how George was going to solve them and save him. George came

up with the most Emperor-like double-cross, which was just incredible and took our breath away. With each character, it's the same thing, constant confrontations, with the twists and turns of fate.

Ian McDiarmid: The Emperor's strength is that he is not fearful, which is of course also young Skywalker's great strength and ultimately Darth Vader's too. It's understanding both sides of fear—how it's important not to be fearful in order to not stop yourself from doing things you believe and know to be right. At the same time, it's on the dark side—terror is what he specializes in. It's what motivates him and governs his every action—his

▶

▶ understanding of the nature of terror. He believes that everybody can be terrorized or seduced by one thing or another. He's only proven wrong at the end of the movie. He doesn't succeed because the father refuses to let him succeed.

Mark Hamill: The philosophy of avoiding confrontation by letting things go and waiting for exactly the right moment to act can be seen in Obi-Wan's actions in Mos Eisley. He tries to avoid trouble. He carries that attitude until the last moment when, if he hadn't acted, Luke would be dead.

Ian McDiarmid: The only emotion that manifests truly is the one seen just before he meets his end—if he does meet his end—and then it's pure anger when he realizes that he hasn't succeeded in manipulating Luke Skywalker. He tries to kill him with unadulterated fury. George

19 / Mark Hamill and Carrie Fisher go before the cameras as the Skywalker siblings give chase through the yet-to-be-added forests of Endor.

20 / Ian McDiarmid as the Emperor.

21 / Sebastian Shaw as the man beneath Darth Vader's mask, Anakin Skywalker.

20 /

director—other actors, cameramen, crew. I was free to choose people whose strengths I knew. We were a team. In the business of making movies, there are no loners. Everyone is working together. There is no one Michelangelo. The effort involves a lot of people mixing paint, preparing the brushes, building the scaffolding, preparing the ceiling, and even doing some sketches around the sides. That's probably how the Sistine Chapel got painted and it's certainly how movies are made.

Ian McDiarmid: I was once chased through a tube station. They were saying, "You've got to stop, you're the Emperor! You've got to stop!" And I managed to run faster than them. They only wanted my autograph. I thought, *This is ridiculous—why don't I just stop and give them my autograph?* But it had gone too far by then.

Billy Dee Williams: I asked George Lucas if I could keep an Ewok head. He looked at me for about ten seconds and said, "Okay."

Kenny Baker: I enjoyed working on *Jedi*. I used to play harmonica and dance with the band at the hotel in Yuma, Arizona. Carrie Fisher would dance with us!

21 /

directed the final sequence when the Emperor is sent down the chute. I won't say killed, because we don't know that, do we…?

Turning, at last, toward the light side of the Force, Darth Vader saves his son from the Emperor's wrath. But the identity of the man beneath the mask, Sebastian Shaw, was unknown, even to his master!

Ian McDiarmid: One day, I happened to see Sebastian Shaw in the corridor at the studio. I knew him quite well, so I said, "Sebastian, what are you doing

here?" He said, "I don't quite know dear boy, but I think it has got something to do with science fiction."

A blockbusting end to the trilogy, the film appeared to bring the stories of Luke Skywalker, Princess Leia, and Han Solo to a close. For the cast and crew, making the trilogy was an experience that would stay with them for many years to come.

Richard Marquand: I was given total carte blanche by George Lucas and the producers in hiring the people that matter to the

Richard Marquand: A lot of people who have tried to do the *Star Wars* thing have not succeeded because they have missed the point. It cannot be campy or put on in any way. It has absolutely got to have that sense of truth.

Mark Hamill: The personal parallels are great. Luke is swept up in the adventures of *Star Wars* just like I was in my career. After *Return of the Jedi*, the question I got asked most often was, "When is the next *Star Wars*?" I wish I had a nickel for every time somebody asked me that. ☺

STAR WARS

RETURN OF THE JEDI

™*

Starring

MARK HAMILL • HARRISON FORD • CARRIE FISHER
BILLY DEE WILLIAMS • ANTHONY DANIELS as C-3PO

Co-starring DAVID PROWSE • KENNY BAKER • PETER MAYHEW • FRANK OZ

Directed by RICHARD MARQUAND   Produced by HOWARD KAZANJIAN

Story by GEORGE LUCAS   Screenplay by LAWRENCE KASDAN and GEORGE LUCAS

Executive Producer GEORGE LUCAS   Music by JOHN WILLIAMS

PG PARENTAL GUIDANCE SUGGESTED
SOME MATERIAL MAY NOT BE SUITABLE FOR CHILDREN

MAY BE TOO INTENSE FOR VERY YOUNG CHILDREN

DO DOLBY STEREO
IN SELECTED THEATRES

ORIGINAL SOUNDTRACK ON RSO RECORDS AND TAPES

A Lucasfilm Ltd. Production — A Twentieth Century-Fox Release
Prints by Deluxe — TM* & © Lucasfilm Ltd (LFL) 1983

NOVELIZATION FROM BALLANTINE BOOKS

STAR WARS: RETURN OF THE JEDI

ESSENTIAL TRIVIA

The film features small roles for Robert Watts (as Lt. Blanaid), Richard Marqaund (as Major. Newland), Ben Burtt (as Dyer) and, in one of her earliest screen roles, award-winning actress Kathy Baker (as a rebel technician).

The word "Ewok" is never said in the film and neither are any of the individual Ewok's names, though they do appear in the end credits.

The lyrics to the Ewok yub nub song (later replaced for the Special Edition) were written by composer John Williams' son, Joseph Williams. Joseph is better known as the lead singer of the band Toto.

The only cast member to shoot new scenes for the 1997 Special Edition was Femi Taylor, who reprised her role of Oola, Jabba's ill-fated dancing girl.

When Princess Leia disguises herself as the bounty hunter Boushh, her voice is provided by Pat Welsh who also voiced E.T.

The film marked the debut of Luke's green lightsaber. A deleted scene showing him building the weapon was included on the Blu-ray release of the film.

In order to preserve secrecy, the film was shot under the title "Blue Harvest" with baseball hats and T-shirts created in order to divert prying eyes.

George Lucas initially wanted Steven Spielberg to direct *Return of the Jedi*.

The Emperor is never named in the film as being Palpatine or Darth Sidious.

Return of the Jedi marks the first time the TIE fighters are mentioned by name.

Return of the Jedi is the only film in the original trilogy in which Darth Vader does not Force choke another character. A scene in which Vader Force chokes Moff Jerjerrod was filmed but ultimately not used.

Peter Mayhew had to be escorted around by crewmembers in the Redwood Forest as there was concern that he would be mistaken for Bigfoot!

Harrison Ford had wanted Han Solo to be killed off but the character was kept alive, until *The Force Awakens*.

Five actors brought Darth Vader/Anakin Skywalker to life. David Prowse and stuntman Bob Anderson wore the suit, James Earl Jones provided the voice, and Sebastian Shaw and Hayden Christensen played Anakin once the helmet was removed.

The shots of Darth Vader's funeral pyre were filmed long after principal photography had been completed.

Sebastian Shaw as the Force spirit of Anakin Skywalker was replaced by Hayden Christensen for the 2004 DVD release and on all subsequent editions of the film.

Carrie Fisher made sure Warwick Davis had milk and cookies between takes.

Ben Kingsley auditioned for the role of the Emperor.

Alan Rickman auditioned for the role of Moff Jerjerrod.

The first scene to be filmed was a sandstorm that the heroes navigate as they leave Tatooine. When Richard Marquand called "Action!" R2-D2 crashed into a rock, the camera team couldn't hear over the wind machines, and the sand obscured almost everything from view.

Actor Dermot Crowley as General Crix Madine had to wear a false beard as the action figure of the character had already been designed as having a beard.

Salacious B. Crumb got his name from two sources: Phil Tippett mangled the word "shoelaces" as "soolacious." The second part of his name came from the cartoonist Robert Crumb.

The cast and crew shared a love of Salacious B. Crumb. "One day, I came in and there was Salacious, and I fell in love with Salacious" said George Lucas. "Salacious is my favorite character. That little character kept me amused during the endless wait between takes," said Anthony Daniels. Stuart Zigg, the chief articulation engineer telexed a message from London to Industrial Light & Magic: "Salacious is stealing the show."

THE SEQUEL TRILOGY

The completion of the acquisition of Lucasfilm by the Disney Corporation in 2013 saw the confirmation that *Star Wars* would be returning to theaters with a new trilogy of movies. The newly appointed president of the company, Kathleen Kennedy, would oversee the movies that saw the return of some familiar faces and a new cast of instantly iconic characters.

Kathleen Kennedy (President of Lucasfilm): Every person who came to the project was a huge *Star Wars* fan. So, that's anybody who grew up with *Star Wars*, like J.J. Abrams and many of the contemporaries that he worked with on the film. Anybody who was post-high school, college age, like me, were still bringing a sense of nostalgia. Then, there were younger people. Some of the people that I was working with on this film never saw the original *Star Wars* in the theater. So, it was a cross-generational group of people bringing all those sensibilities to the making of this movie. It made you feel like you're in this with so many people who genuinely cared about it, that it's all going to be okay.

The fans were sitting out there wondering what we're going to do with it, and everybody inside the process is a fan. So, you've extended out to this community that is becoming a part of making the movie. So, even though there was no guarantee, and there was stress and expectation, it was something we genuinely felt that we were in together.

It was nice to be involved in a movie that everyone cares so much about. It's not just that they care because they're fans, but *Star Wars* has had something to do with their life. It's something they've drawn from. It's the reason they got into the movie business. That means that their passion will show up on the screen.

2 /

In the run-up to the film, a worldwide audition process was undertaken as the filmmakers looked for a young woman to play the lead, Rey.

Daisy Ridley (Rey): I have no idea what I did. I just tried very hard and I hoped very much. There wasn't much advice offered—there was a conversation with Harrison Ford about anonymity, but really it was just people leading by example. It was amazing to see people who are so established and with a huge career being kind and generous to everyone on set.

Harrison Ford and Peter Mayhew found themselves reunited as Han Solo and Chewbacca. The *Millennium Falcon* crew were glad to be reacquainted with their ship.

Harrison Ford (Han Solo): I didn't remember it as well as I thought I did. There are things I remember about the cockpit and

3 /

1 / J.J. Abrams directs Daisy Ridley in her movie debut. (Previous spread)

2 / Daisy Ridley, John Boyega, and Harrison Ford film a scene with Lupita Nyong'o in Maz Kanata's castle.

3 / J.J. Abrams directs John Boyega as Finn turns his back on the First Order.

the funny stuff we went through. On the original cockpit, I asked George Lucas to let us get into it, so we could try it on for size. Finally, we did get a chance, Chewbacca [Peter Mayhew] and I, to walk into the cockpit. Of course, he couldn't get into the seat! Flying it developed a little bit between iterations of the first three films, but it started to come back to me. It was fun.

Peter Mayhew (Chewbacca):
One person's idea of perfect is not everybody's. But, when I saw it, I thought, *Yeah, this is back. This is what it looked like when we shot the original films.*

J.J. Abrams (Director, writer):
The *Millennium Falcon* is as much a returning character in the film as the people. There's a very weird feeling going back to something you know so well. It's like saying, "I'm going to open this magic door and, behind this magic door is your bedroom at nine years old." You can walk into that bedroom and you can feel it, and smell it, and open drawers in your desk, and find the things you had. What would be in that desk? What would be under your bed? That feeling of, it's yours, and you know it. So, when you go back to it, it has to look like what you remember.

So, we made sure we almost forensically recreated the *Falcon*. We had the most incredible crew. Our art director, Mark Harris, who worked on *The Empire Strikes Back*, was like a scientist figuring out how the *Falcon* changed from *A New Hope* to *Empire*. The size of the cockpit expanded, and the scale of the ship got bigger in the second film. We realized that with the stuff you thought was canon, big changes were being made. You can't adhere to what you think it was, and do what they did. If something needs adjusting, do it. But, aesthetically, it can't look or sound different than the ship you know. An incredible number of hours were put into it, and making it as we know it.

▶

4 /

5 /

6 /

▶ Also making a long-awaited return to the saga was Carrie Fisher as General Leia Organa.

Carrie Fisher (General Leia Organa): J.J. was great to work with because he talks a lot. And it's really good stuff that he says, so that was exciting to hear. He remembers everyone's name and he's got a lot of energy. He was really excited to direct the film, because he was young when I was a teenager and so he was sort of a fan! It was infectious excitement and real focus, because he has high verbal acuity. And he really loved making the movie. Except with me!

The script called for a new kind of villain, a complex figure torn between the light and dark side of the Force.

Adam Driver (Kylo Ren): The idea of doing [this film] was a scary thing. Even though J.J. mapped out what that character does, he left out a lot of things for us to discover. He wanted to get my input, which was a huge thing also in a movie of this scale. Suddenly, you have a director who wants you to be involved in making it, and given the history of these movies, that's very exciting. I was a fan of the *Star Wars* movies when I was younger, so suddenly to

4 / J.J. Abrams and Oscar Isaac line up a shot.

5 / Joonas Suotamo and Harrison Ford work out a scene with Abrams.

6 / Han Solo in action!

7 / Rey and Kylo Ren duel on the surface of Starkiller Base.

8 / Harrison Ford and Joonas Suotamo on the Starkiller Base set. (Overleaf)

work on it in my adult life and have input seems unbelievable.

Joining Kylo Ren in the First Order, Captain Phasma gave the saga a new icon and its first on-screen female villain.

Gwendoline Christie (Captain Phasma): The costume was so brilliantly designed by Michael Kaplan, who I've admired since I saw his work on *Blade Runner* (1982) when I was twelve years old. I was really astounded by how extraordinary Phasma's armor looked and how practical it was to wear. I love the fact ▶

▶ that the costume hadn't been feminized or sexualized in any way. It's practical armor. What I got from the costume was that this was a woman who was imposing, uncompromising, and high-functioning. That informs the way that I moved, and the way that I walked. It all goes to communicate something about the character.

John Boyega played Finn, a stormtrooper-turned-deserter once commanded by Captain Phasma, until he refused to fire on civilians. The actor soon felt the heat of being in a *Star Wars* film.

John Boyega (Finn): Abu Dhabi is a beautiful place. We were there to shoot the first part of the movie. I'm in this nice hotel and I get in my car and as we're driving, I'm looking all around at the structure of Abu Dhabi. It looks amazing. We ended up in the desert where the TIE fighter scene was being shot. When I walked on to the set, I saw this huge, life-size TIE fighter, black and red, crushed in the sand. Balls of fire everywhere. Debris. TIE fighter skid marks going 200 yards. And, of course, Finn has to be in a stormtrooper outfit. I had to wear it in this heat for the next couple of days. Let's just say I relied on a combination of sweat, passion, fandom, ice cubes, eye drops, and a lot of water. I was drenched in sweat by the time I got out of the stormtrooper outfit. But, most days, it got easier based on passion and fandom alone. I was trying to be professional but every time J.J.

10

Abrams would come up to me with a note, I'd be like, "It's a TIE fighter!" I was literally star-struck seeing a TIE fighter next to me. It made the scenes easier, though the conditions were very hot.

Originally ear-marked to die during his crash landing on Jakku, Oscar Isaac relished his role as hot shot pilot Poe Dameron.

Oscar Isaac (Poe Dameron): It's a real textured world and environment. We actually have two full-sized X-wings standing there that you can run up to and the cockpit will open! You can jump inside and fire them up. Everyone that's involved feels like it's real and like it's there. It infuses the film with something that's unquantifiable. It's unlike anything I've done before.

What I like about it, too, is that it's also a bit of a period piece because it goes back to the technology that they were using in the original films. There is a slightly 1980s vibe that they're able to elicit with a lot of the designs and using actual everyday objects as well

9 / Andy Serkis wears his motion-capture suit as he performs as Snoke.

10 / John Boyega feels the heat in Abu Dhabi.

11 / Daisy Ridley goes before the camera as Rey rides her speeder.

mixed into the set. That's just so great because, again, it's a reminder that it is part of a legacy and a culture. You're creating culture. That's something that Max von Sydow [Lor San Tekka] had said when we were sitting there talking a little bit. He said these movies create culture; they create a whole lineage and ancestry with all these little bits and pieces that they use. It infuses everything with meaning.

Continuing his unbroken run of appearing in all of the Skywalker saga films, Anthony Daniels returned as C-3PO.

Anthony Daniels (C-3PO): On any film set, but particularly with this one, there is an extraordinary feeling of collaboration. You have so many different departments, whether it's props, makeup, costume, wardrobe, green screen, set dressers, electricians, lighting, camera, sound, or acting. J.J. has created a collaborative experience. I think everybody feels the ability to walk up and say, "Can we try that?" Obviously, you can't waste ▶

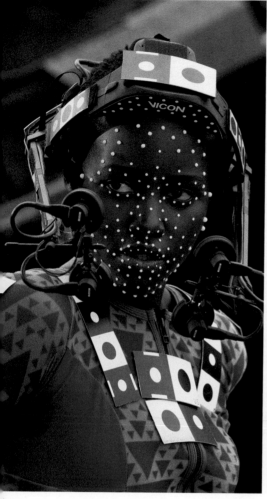

▶ the director's entire day, but he's created an atmosphere where everybody can offer something.

Commanding the First Order is Supreme Leader Snoke and General Hux, with the former brought to life by an actor who is no stranger to performance capture.

Andy Serkis (Supreme Leader Snoke): Performance capture is the art and craft of an actor embodying a role that will be manifested on screen as a computer-generated character. But the authorship of the role, all the acting, takes place with other actors. Instead of putting on a costume and makeup beforehand, you're playing the role without the help of those things, but neither

the hindrance. All of the facial expressions, all your acting decisions, and the authorship of the role happen on set with the other actors. A clever team of animators and CG artists then have the job of transposing that performance onto a digital avatar without losing the nuance and subtlety and underlying performance of what the actor has given. That's how motion capture works. What's amazing is that it enables anyone to play anything. Philosophically, it's the greatest acting tool of the 21st century. It doesn't matter what size you are. Stereotyping, or typecasting, is dead. It doesn't matter what the color of your skin or your height or your sex is. It's a brilliantly liberating tool that

actors are finally seeing, and the more it's used as a standard industry tool, it's really proliferated.

Domhnall Gleeson (General Hux): The costume designer, Michael Kaplan did an amazing job with the costumes. It absolutely feels like *Star Wars*. You look around and you immediately know what universe you're in. You wouldn't have to just look at the set because if you look at the costumes, you'd immediately recognize the world. But, it's also slightly different than what they did before. Hux has to carry an aura of power and a preoccupation of being in charge of things. The clothes correct your posture. So, it's been ▶

12 / Adam Driver goes before the camera as the sinister Kylo Ren.

13 / Lupita Nyong'o dons a motion-capture suit as Maz Kanata comes to life.

14 / First Order officer General Hux (Domhnall Gleeson).

15 / J.J. Abrams and Lawrence Kasdan have a script conference on set.

16 / John Boyega shares a drink with a happabore as Abrams directs. (Overleaf)

17 /

▶ brilliant and hilarious to put on those clothes every morning.

Portraying the playful, mysterious Maz Kanata was Lupita Nyong'o, using performance capture to create a unique new character.

Lupita Nyong'o (Maz Kanata): A typical day for me on set involves coming into makeup— actually for the dots! There are 149 dots put on my face every morning. We got it down to between forty-five minutes to an hour, depending on how cooperative the glue is being. I suit up, and then I have markers. My suit is gray with triangles everywhere, then I have markers that make it look like a road sign is velcroed onto the suit. Then, a headcam is put on my head with four cameras that shine a ring of LED lights onto my face to capture every movement my face makes. Then, we begin...

The first time I came onto set in that suit, it was the most alienating thing in the world. Because there are lights shining on my face, everyone is drawn to look at me. I was fighting nerves, butterflies in my stomach, and feeling very self-conscious! I was still trying to figure out how to be this completely different person in this suit and to have an understanding of my physicality and the space around me. It was bizarre.

For writer Lawrence Kasdan, *The Force Awakens* had one goal.

Lawrence Kasdan: I used one word from the beginning, it must "delight." When you have John Williams writing the music, you're part of the way there. When you have this group of craftspeople creating the images, you're part of the way there. When [director of photography] Dan Mindel shoots a movie, you're going to be delighted and when J.J. directs a movie, you'll be delighted, and we will have succeeded. ☺

18 /

20 /

17 / Finn, BB-8,
and Rey aboard the
Millennium Falcon.

18 / Rey and Han Solo
join forces.

19 / Stranded on
Jakku, Rey's destiny
lies elsewhere.

20 / General Leia
Organa, selfless leader
of the Resistance.

STAR WARS
THE FORCE AWAKENS

A LUCASFILM LTD. PRODUCTION A BAD ROBOT PRODUCTION "STAR WARS: THE FORCE AWAKENS" HARRISON FORD MARK HAMILL CARRIE FISHER ADAM DRIVER
DAISY RIDLEY JOHN BOYEGA OSCAR ISAAC LUPITA NYONG'O ANDY SERKIS DOMHNALL GLEESON ANTHONY DANIELS PETER MAYHEW and MAX VON SYDOW MUSIC BY JOHN WILLIAMS
VISUAL EFFECTS & ANIMATION BY INDUSTRIAL LIGHT & MAGIC COSTUME DESIGNER MICHAEL KAPLAN EDITORS MARY JO MARKEY, ACE MARYANN BRANDON, ACE PRODUCTION DESIGNERS RICK CARTER and DARREN GILFORD DIRECTOR OF PHOTOGRAPHY DAN MINDEL, ASC, BSC
EXECUTIVE PRODUCERS TOMMY HARPER JASON McGATLIN PRODUCED BY KATHLEEN KENNEDY, p.g.a. J.J. ABRAMS, p.g.a. BRYAN BURK, p.g.a. WRITTEN BY LAWRENCE KASDAN & J.J. ABRAMS and MICHAEL ARNDT DIRECTED BY J.J. ABRAMS

  SOUNDTRACK AVAILABLE ON Walt Disney RECORDS StarWars.com/TheForceAwakens

DECEMBER 18
IN 3D, REAL D 3D AND IMAX 3D

LUCASFILM Ltd

STAR WARS: THE FORCE AWAKENS

ESSENTIAL TRIVIA

Director J.J. Abrams chose the name BB-8 because he looked round and bouncy. He said, "I named him BB-8 because it was almost onomatopoeia… It was sort of how he looked to me, with the eight, obviously, and then the two Bs."

According to the *The Force Awakens Visual Dictionary*, Captain Phasma's armor is coated in salvaged chromium from a Naboo yacht once owned by Emperor Palpatine.

Finn, whose trooper designation is FN-2187, is a reference created by director J.J. Abrams to Princess Leia's cell number, 2187, aboard the Death Star in *A New Hope*. It was originally a reference George Lucas was making to the 1963 short film *21-87*.

Rey's goggles are cobbled together using a pair of lenses from a stormtrooper's helmet.

When Poe Dameron first wakes up, bound to an interrogation table on the *Finalizer*, the sound of an IT-000 droid can be heard—it's just behind Kylo Ren in the scene. An earlier model of this droid, the IT-O Interrogation Unit, was used by Darth Vader in an effort to force Princess Leia to reveal the location of the rebel base.

Carrie Fisher's daughter, Billie Lourd, plays Lieutenant Connix, who appears in the Resistance base on D'Qar. She would also appear in *The Last Jedi* and *The Rise of Skywalker*.

The hologram dejarik set seen on the *Millennium Falcon* was animated by Tippett Studios, which is owned and supervised by the same special effects mastermind who worked on the original sequence in *A New Hope*, Phil Tippett.

The flags at Maz Kanata's castle are imprinted with familiar images from the *Star Wars* films and cartoons, including the skull from Boba Fett's left-shoulder blast plate, Hondo Ohnaka's gang symbol, Ziro the Hutt's belly tattoo from *The Clone Wars*, and Cikatro Vizago's Broken Horn Syndicate symbol from *Rebels*. There is even a flag displaying the universal symbol for the 501st, an organization of fans who do charitable work in costume, mainly as stormtroopers.

Composer and actor Lin-Manuel Miranda, most recently of *Hamilton: An American Musical* fame, wrote the tracks "Jabba Flow" and "Dobra Doompa," which were performed at Maz Kanata's castle.

In addition to his role as translator, C-3PO is in charge of a pool of droids across the galaxy, including GA-97, who reports BB-8's presence at Maz Kanata's castle.

James Bond actor Daniel Craig makes a cameo appearance in *The Force Awakens*. He plays a stormtrooper who falls victim to Rey's Jedi Mind Trick on Starkiller Base.

Kylo Ren's interrogation of Poe Dameron on Jakku was one of the first scenes to be shot. J.J. Abrams went back and added some humor to the scene in reshoots, with Poe saying "I can't understand you with that mask on."

The beginning of Rey's Force vision brings her to a hallway in *The Empire Strikes Back* that led to the catwalk where Darth Vader faced his son.

During Rey's Force vision, or "Forceback," at Maz's castle, many voices and sounds are heard, including Darth Vader's breathing and Yoda explaining the nature of the Force. The sound designers took the word "afraid" and altered it to sound like "Rey." They then combined that with a new voice-over from actor Ewan McGregor to complete the line, "Rey… these are your first steps."

Actress Harriet Walter plays Doctor Kalonia, the physician who treated Chewie's wounds after the engagement at Takodana. In addition to *The Force Awakens*, Walter has appeared as Lady Shackleton on *Downtown Abbey*. She is also the niece of Christopher Lee, who played Count Dooku in *Attack of the Clones* and *Revenge of the Sith*.

In the first version of his initial scene with Snoke, Kylo Ren was not wearing his mask. J.J. Abrams had the scene digitally altered in post-production to put the mask on him so that Adam Driver's face could be revealed later the movie.

Following the enormous box office success of *Star Wars: The Force Awakens* was no easy task, but Rian Johnson helmed a film that took the *Star Wars* saga into unexpected territories. The story picked up as Rey confronted Luke Skywalker on that mountainside on Ahch-To…

Alan Horn (Co-Chairman, Walt Disney Studios): Rian Johnson is a cinephile. He really knows film and he has a great eye. He carries a camera with him everywhere and takes pictures of everything. The film was mostly cast before he took the picture. But he's so relatable and comfortable that I think the cast really responded to him. The good thing about Rian is, not only did he direct the picture, he wrote it. He's a true auteur.

Rian Johnson (Writer/Director): Some of my earliest memories of creative play, of telling my own stories, were with *Star Wars* toys and in that universe, but there was much more fear and trepidation at the weight of actually working on a real *Star Wars* film. If I had let myself zoom back and look at the enormity of the task, and the responsibility of it, I would have just been paralyzed and spent the last few years curled up in the fetal position.

I asked the questions: *What do I think the characters want? Where can I see them going? And what would be the hardest thing for each of them to come up against?* And once I got to a place where I had something for each one of them that made sense, I started drawing it out into a story. It's kind of like eating an elephant. You just do it one bite at a time.

Kathleen Kennedy (President of Lucasfilm): Rian writes amazingly fierce and independent women, and has a great sense of humor, which is so vital to the character of *Star Wars*. He observes human behavior really well. He's got a very good heart and a real soul to what he does. A filmmaker's particular style and vision is what shapes these stories, and that shines through in Rian's film.

Ram Bergman (Producer): For Rian, it is always about the characters. He was able to come up with a story that was powerful and emotional and goes in an unexpected way. The story is what is true for the characters; it takes them on a journey that feels real.

Rian Johnson: One of the first things that Kathleen Kennedy told me when she asked me if I'd be interested in doing this was that the lead character was a girl named Rey. I was instantly into that; it just felt right. Leia was the first female figure that girls and women could look up to, and seeing how much it meant to them, Carrie Fisher was very conscious of that and held that with her. She felt a responsibility to make Leia great. I was really interested in the strong and powerful and weak and conflicted and good and bad female characters—portrayed by an amazing array of actors. There are a lot of kick-ass women in this movie.

Ram Bergman: Rian and I had worked on a few drafts before we submitted a version we were happy with to Kathleen Kennedy. Rian thought it was a small movie, and I didn't necessarily think it was that big a movie. Kathleen called me to say how much she loved the script and that this is a giant movie! She said, "How are you going to do this?"

When we really started diving into it, we realized the scope was really big. Fortunately, Rian was able to deliver the script a year in advance, so we had a lot of time to figure out what we needed to make the film. It wasn't that hard. If you have someone like Rian ▶

1 / Rey (Daisy Ridley) on the island home of Luke Skywalker, Ahch-To. (Previous spread)

2 / Rian Johnson directs Joonas Suomato (Chewbacca) aboard the *Millennium Falcon*.

3 / Kelly Marie Tran (Rose) and John Boyega (Finn) rehearse with Rian Johnson.

4 / Johnson directs John Boyega and Oscar Isaac (Poe Dameron).

3 /

▶ who has a clear vision that he can articulate, it makes the process easier. When the project is driven by somebody who can write, direct, and knows every element and aesthetic that he wants, with the best people in the world working for you, that's the biggest part of it.

Mark Hamill (Luke Skywalker): At first, when I read the script [for *The Last Jedi*], I thought, *This is really pushing me out of my comfort zone.* We've seen benign, wise Jedi before, and nobody can do it better than Alec Guinness. But I think being pushed out of my comfort zone was a good thing.

Daisy Ridley (Rey): Mark [Hamill] and I have both talked about our unexpected reactions to reading *The Last Jedi*. We were very lucky that we had a couple weeks rehearsal with Rian where we could just talk through everything. Working with a new director and a new co-star is pretty big stuff. I felt like we were

working through an actual relationship. I seem to remember it working chronologically—or at least it seemed to in my mind. As our relationship was growing, the characters' relationship was growing, as you see it on-screen.

After his brief cameo in *The Force Awakens*, Mark Hamill was particularly impressed to be working with a talented cast.

Mark Hamill: The cast is spectacular; everyone is so talented in their own way. I felt a strong sense of nostalgia! I used to be the orphan discovery with hidden powers, now we've got Rey. I used to be the hotshot, impulsive X-wing fighter pilot, now we've got Poe Dameron. I used to be the one sneaking around enemy territory in disguise, now we've got Rose and Finn. So I had to fight the irrational urge that it's a bunch of strangers rummaging through my old toy box playing with my old toys! But basically now, at this age, I'm happy to let the kids do the heavy lifting.

6 /

One of the biggest puzzles Rian Johnson had to solve was establishing why Luke Skywalker had taken himself into exile.

Rian Johnson: I knew Luke Skywalker was not a coward and I knew he was not hiding. I knew if he's there, he's taken himself out of the fight, and he must have a reason for doing that... But why?

Mark Hamill: Because of the gravity of the situation—the urgency of the situation—Rey doesn't have the luxury of getting to know him and relax and exchange ideas. She needs him and wants to enlist his help and abilities to her cause. And that's the conflict. Luke's in a very different place than we've ever seen him before. Luke always represented hope and optimism. And now, here he is pessimistic, disillusioned, and demoralized.

Daisy Ridley: In this movie, Rey is learning not to believe the hype. Good people make bad choices, and bad people can make good choices. She's learning her own strengths and weaknesses and continuing to learn about the human psyche, because she hasn't really had relationships with people before. Rey doesn't see herself as this powerful being and seeing Luke is a reflection of what people see her as. They talk about her potential, and she doesn't really feel it. But she does start to come around. She tries to move forward and do the right thing, like she has always done.

Rian Johnson: I think she probably expects there are some answers about who she is, and that's really what she is on a quest to find out. Not just meaning who her parents are or where she comes from, but meaning what's her place in all of this? When she shows up on that island, there's part of her, and there's a big part of us, that expects that she's going to get that information from Luke.

7 /

5 / The lost Jedi, Luke Skywalker (Mark Hamill) in exile.

6 / Ram Bergman, Rian Johnson, and Kathleen Kennedy share a light moment on set.

7 / Rey uses the Force to aid the Resistance as the First Order ▶ closes in.

▶ Daisy Ridley: I like that I never questioned being a heroic woman in a film, and that's thanks to my upbringing. My mom's always worked; the women I grew up around always worked and were inspirational. So it's weird because the way people reacted made me question more than I did. It's a great role but not just because she's a woman. That's how simple it was to me. But others were like, "This is a big deal," clearly. It's exciting to be a part of that, and I'm thinking, *Let's continue*. This is how it should be.

A key sequence in the movie saw Luke confronting a piece of his past: the *Millennium Falcon*.

Mark Hamill: Stepping onto the *Millennium Falcon* set was bittersweet. It's like going to your old high school or the house you lived in in sixth grade. The detail was perfect. It's just as I remembered it. I climbed up and down the ladder, got in the hold where we stowed away, and sat in the cockpit with my grown children and wife. Later, I slipped away and got really choked up. This is a moment, and it'll be gone.

The movie picked up the story of the Resistance as General Organa led the retreat from the First Order, helped and hindered by Poe Dameron.

Carrie Fisher (General Leia Organa): Leia has gone from being someone who's shooting guns and swinging across chasms and killing Jabba the Hutt, to being serious, and worrying a lot. She has a lot more responsibility and there's a plenty of reasons for her to be exhausted.

Our relationships in the movie are very much like our relationships in life. We take care of each other, in a way. Poe is Leia's protégé, and in a way, she thinks of him as Han, which is both the good news and the bad news. He's dominating and he doesn't listen to her. She's trying to train him.

8 / Rian Johnson confers with Carrie Fisher (General Leia Organa) on set.

9 / Leia offers guidance to Poe Dameron (Oscar Isaac).

10 / Poe Dameron stages a mutiny!

9 /

deal with being grounded. Poe is learning to not just be a soldier but to be a leader. Not just be the heroic pilot but perhaps learn to be a general. And that's a shift. He's a man on a mission. You give him a mission, and he'll complete it. But seeing the bigger picture, knowing when not to engage, that's what he has to learn.

The film introduced a new character, Rose Tico, who joins forces with Finn on a daring mission.

Kelly Marie Tran (Rose Tico): I'll remember the moments we had on set for the rest of my life. This was my first substantial role in a very large movie. I just loved that Rian had this sort of child-like wonder about everything. Everything felt fun, and then you'd be doing a scene and hear his little laugh, and I'd think, *We're doing it, we're doing it!* It just felt like we were hanging out in someone's backyard making a movie for ourselves. And I think that's really special.

Rian Johnson: Rose Tico is the closest to how ten-year-old me would have felt if he woke up in this universe. She doesn't belong here, but she's going to be brave and do her best. Luckily, we found the perfect embodiment of that spirit with Kelly Marie Tran. I love her to death, and I was thrilled to introduce audiences to both Rose and Kelly.

Kelly Marie Tran: Rose works in maintenance, and she's a nobody. Her sister's always been the cool one that's been out there in the forefront of the action. Rose has always been the one behind pipes, fixing things. Finn is a big deal to her, like a childhood hero. Rose has always been someone who has been on the bottom of the food chain in the Resistance. And here is Finn, someone who, for her, represents why she's there. So they meet and go on a series of crazy adventures together.

Oscar Isaac (Poe Dameron): I like Rian's laid-back attitude. I'd describe him as a West Coast jazz musician. He just hangs back. He's fast but so mellow, and with all that craziness going on too! I remember when we were reading the script in Rian's office with Carrie Fisher. We were just improvising and trying all sorts of crazy stuff to figure out how to play those scenes. There was a real looseness to it within all of the wildness.

I was really excited to see what kind of role Rian created for Poe in the story. The conflict he has to deal with is brutal. He took away the one thing that Poe knows how to do so well—jumping into an X-wing and blowing things up—so Poe had to

▶ **John Boyega (Finn):** Finn is motivated by personal emotion, not by ideological causes. His bravery in *The Force Awakens* is to save his friend, not because he cares about her cause or Poe's army. In *The Last Jedi,* we went deeper in and see what he really believes in when the rubber meets the road. Finn and Rose are two people who are thrown together by circumstance and fate. They make a really good team.

With General Leia injured following an attack by the First Order, the Resistance is placed under command of Vice Admiral Holdo, played by acclaimed actress Laura Dern.

Laura Dern (Vice Admiral Holdo): It's deeply important that Holdo was so feminine and so in control. We all felt that a leader should be able to be feminine and not have to be one of the boys to lead. I thought that was a great choice in terms of the design, the hair, and the costume.

It felt protective, safe, and collaborative. It was like an independent movie in a way. Periodically, I'd look up and see Chewbacca or Artoo-Detoo

walking by, which reminded me of what I was doing! It was the best party I've been invited to.

Michael Kaplan (Costume Designer): Rian wanted Holdo to be more independently dressed. "Balletic"as the word he used, to show off her body, something she could be flirtatious in. A gown but one that had authority and presence.

Oscar Isaac: I was fortunate to have so many scenes with Laura. We were on set in our jeans and T-shirts, rehearsing, and talking about our different motivations. Just to take that kind of time in such a huge movie is pretty special. I was really happy with that, and also, of course, very happy to be working with Carrie again.

Among the classic characters to return was Chewbacca, played for the first time by Joonas Suotamo, stepping into Peter Mayhew's shoes.

Joonas Suotamo (Chewbacca): I did miss working with Harrison Ford. He was so much fun on set, and he kept me in my place! He was very serious about being Han Solo.

A small break occurred in filming when Princes William and Harry toured the Pinewood set, and *Star Wars*' most famous siblings took the chance to ask some questions.

Mark Hamill: I used the opportunity when the princes came for a tour to solve something that had been bothering me since 1982. When George Lucas told us that Carrie and I were brother and sister, I said, "Wait a minute, if Luke's Princess Leia's brother, doesn't that make me royalty?" Carrie said, "No!"

When I met the princes, I said, "My mother was Queen Amidala, my father was Lord Vader, my sister is Princess Leia. Doesn't that make me royalty?" Unfortunately, it was a split decision. William said yes, Harry said he needed more information!

Daisy Ridley: There are so many people involved in the making of the film who have worked far longer and far harder than the actors. To be able to take the princes to the creature workshop, and the props and costumes departments—where people aren't always publicly recognized for the work they do—felt pretty cool.   ▶

11 / Rey and Chewbacca
(Joonas Suomato) pilot
the *Millennium Falcon*.

12 / Rose and Finn
witness decadance
at the galaxy's expense
at Canto Bight.

13 / Vice Admiral
Holdo (Laura Dern)
deals with mutiny in the
Resistance.

13 /

▶ Commanding the First Order, Andy Serkis and Domhnall Gleeson returned as Supreme Leader Snoke and General Hux.

Andy Serkis (Supreme Leader Snoke): I had to identify with Snoke in some way. I don't believe in the concept of pure evil, but I think we're all capable of incredible darkness, as well as incredible creativity and love. So you have to look honestly at yourself and think: *What part is there I can possibly connect to?* That's your job as an actor. You have to use your imagination to find that part of you. We all have to admit what we're capable of. It's very important to try and humanize "evil characters" in some way. There's a vulnerability we tried to approach that is born out of fear—fear that the First Order is in a pretty shoddy state, and not being handled terribly well by Hux and Kylo Ren. The thing about Snoke is that there's this public hologram appearance he uses to scare people, and then there's the wizard behind the curtain. He's quite frail and fearful because he dreads the powerful feminine energy that he knows is coming to take him down.

Domhnall Gleeson (General Hux): As an actor, I'm on Hux's side when I'm playing him. He wants order in the galaxy, he thinks things are out of control, he's scared of the Force—I think he probably has a point! There's lots about him that I understand, but there are also a few things that are probably not the best! Rian and I talked about the idea of Hux being like a kicked dog, because he's kind of undermined in the film, but we don't lose the idea of him being able to cause some damage. We talked about a dog who gets kicked over and over again, and how he is eventually going to bite back.

14 / Adam Driver (Kylo Ren) rehearses the battle with Supreme Leader Snoke's guards while Rian Johnson checks the angles.

15 / General Hux (Domhnall Gleeson) contemplates his next duplicitous move.

16 / Finn settles an old score with his former commander, Captain Phasma (Gwendoline Christie).

17 / Kylo Ren at his most dangerous and unpredictable.

The demands of the movie's action sequences meant that the cast had to train hard before picking up their lightsabers.

Daisy Ridley: It was so rigorous, but I enjoyed pushing myself. It's amazing what you can do. The big fight with Kylo Ren and Snoke's guards involved a lot of stamina. It took two weeks to shoot. It was hard work just to keep up with everything. I think that if I just learned the choreography, that wasn't really doing it justice. I had to fight and act. I hadn't been working out, as such, in the year between *The Force Awakens* and *The Last Jedi*—I'd been strength training. When we got back into filming, we didn't have the time to train that we had the first time around, but I felt stronger. I have to say, I felt pretty badass!

For John Boyega, a highlight of the film was a chance for Finn to settle the score with his old boss.

John Boyega (Finn): The fight with Phasma was a challenge, because the weapon was different for me this time. There was a lot of stunt training, mostly with Gwendoline [Christie], and she has a really strong reach. I needed to dodge and pirouette around her at all times.

15 /

16 /

18 /

▶ A visit to the luxuriant casino featured a menagerie of creatures and aliens.

Rian Johnson: Canto Bight was a Monte Carlo-like city that had to dazzle and seduce us. It was by far the most involved design process in the movie. Rick Heinrichs and his team worked to fuse visual cues from *Star Wars* into an entirely new feeling of wealth and opulence.

Neal Scanlan (Creature Effects): We're used to seeing the grungier side of *Star Wars*, but less used to seeing the high rollers of the galaxy. It was quite a trick to hold on to the *Star Wars* DNA while taking it to a place we hadn't been to before. It is the

final confirmation at every level. That's the first time we got to step back and see not only our department, but all the other departments' aspirations and vision for the film come together. There can't be many people who didn't walk on that set and take a breath. From the set to the props, everything about it was incredible.

Rick Heinrichs (Production Designer): Canto Bight is an extremely extravagant, over-the-top version of Monte Carlo. We used a lot of architectural references to earlier *Star Wars* films, like columns and arches, but with more ovular, circular, softer shapes than what we've seen in the

other films. I had read that Ralph McQuarrie, when he was working on Jabba's palace, realized that if he kept with rectilinear forms, it would look like a black castle from some 1930s swashbuckling movie. However, if he kept to soft deco shapes, there's a real opportunity to come up with something fresh, an opulent quality, which would convey the idea of fun and beauty. That's what we were aiming for.

John Boyega: On set I was like a twelve-year-old kid at Disneyland, but Disneyland was on level ten. That's just what it was like, but then you had to do your job because you were part of the story. I tried to take it all in as a fan whilst remaining professional about my role in the

19 /

film. Ultimately, I think I did well with the balance, but it was crazy because there was so much going on. There were both major sets and practical effects to navigate. The crew outdid themselves with the sets they built. It made me feel like I was on another planet, which was good.

Michael Kaplan: We chose extras based on sophistication, good posture, and exoticism. We were able to design costumes specifically for the individuals we'd chosen.

Peter Swords King (Makeup): A lot we pushed out because they just weren't *Star Wars*-looking enough. They didn't look intergalactic or were too ordinary. We were looking for extraordinary, almost impractical, impossible hairstyles and makeup. It took us about six months to get all these styles and looks whittled down. A good third of the women had all their eyebrows blocked out. We didn't put new ones in. And it just makes them look strange. If you take someone's eyebrows away, it's the oddest thing. It was designing with concept designers, scrolling through books, taking influence from the 1960s and 70s and adapting those. But then, just some really crazy, wacky ideas. It was brilliant fun.

During their adventure on Canto Bight, Finn and Rose meet the mysterious "DJ," an ally as long as it suits him.

Benicio Del Toro (DJ):
DJ believes that good guys and bad guys are just basically the same. He's a profiteer. He profits from the eternal war of good and evil. He's an opportunist but can get you out of a jam, and get you in a jam. We played that line of whether he is good or bad. We don't know. But he's a mercenary, really.

Rian Johnson: DJ's mantra is live free and don't join. He shows Finn that even the good guys are dirty at times and perhaps corrupt as well. He's like this little devil on Finn's shoulder that basically is trying to make him see a different side or different approach to living in the galaxy.

The finale takes place on the mineral world of Crait, a strange new environment that features some unique creatures.

Rian Johnson: Crait has a thin, white layer of salt that's like a topsoil, but under that is a ruby-red crystal foundation. It offered incredible possibilities for an alien environment that we hadn't seen before. ▶

20 /

Neal Scanlan: We had a taxidermy form of a fox and created a clay sculpture that we added straw to, in order to see how you'd replace hair. Then, we tried to find a balance between something that was solid and heavy but also soft and appealing. Rian kept pushing us toward making them sparkle, with a more crystal-like appearance. I saw the vulptices as a predominantly female species.

John Williams added some Easter eggs to his epic musical score…

John Williams (Composer): I won't give them away, but there are a couple of really fun inside jokes about how we've disguised some old music that Rian wanted to place here and there. I'll leave the viewers to discover it—or ignore it as they wish—but we had a playful time with it as well.

The cast and crew were saddened to learn of the death of Carrie Fisher, who passed away in December, 2016.

Rian Johnson: First and foremost, Carrie was a writer, and that's how we first really connected. We had a lot of really nice moments on set, but the times I remember her best were when we were hanging out at her house before the shoot. She was digging out books for me that she wanted to talk about. She was writing *The Princess Diarist* when we were filming, and she showed me all the diaries from 1976. I feel really lucky to have had a little bit of time to know her.

Ram Bergman: Carrie had a meaningful role in the film even before her untimely death, but now there is so much more weight to some very emotional scenes. She challenged Rian every day, but they had a great partnership. Everyone was so proud of her performance.

Dohmnall Gleeson: Carrie was really cool about coming up to people, and not making it a thing to have to approach her and say "Hi, I'm in the film, can I say hello?" The magic of film is that you live forever. For people who knew Carrie, she'll live forever to them anyway. She was so kind, and as irreverent as anybody I've ever met in my life. Nobody knew

21 /

20 / Kylo commands the First Order to annihilate Luke Skywalker!

21 / The First Order troops pursue the Resistance.

22 / Poe Dameron leads the desperate fight back.

23 / Luke Skywalker faces his former apprentice on Crait.

what was going to happen with Carrie. I love that Rian wrote her a beautiful film.

The Last Jedi proved to a box office smash, leaving fans keen to see where the story would go next.

Daisy Ridley: Even though this is the second episode in this series, it's its own thing without just leading onto the next one, which is great.

Mark Hamill: If you look at Rian's movies, each is different than the

last. You can't pigeonhole him and say, "That's the kind of film he makes." *The Last Jedi* is so different in many ways, subtle ways, than the other *Star Wars* movies, and yet it is satisfying in delivering what the fans want to see as well.

Rian Johnson: I had the time of my life making this movie. In many ways it felt the closest I've ever gotten to a professional equivalent of that freewheeling play, being a kid and running around the room with action figures.

Alan Horn: There's an accumulated affection and expectation with the fans as we go forward. George Lucas started it, and J.J. Abrams did a wonderful job of carrying it on. I'm thrilled with the work of Rian Johnson. His vision will last forever.

Carrie Fisher: For me, it's about family. That's what is so powerful about it. I go to Comic-Con and meet a lot of these people and it's very powerful for them. They're showing the films to their children

and their grandchildren. They're sharing something that moved them as a child. That's personal. I've watched a lot of that over the years, like people coming in with babies that have the Princess Leia outfit on. That's the thing that makes it so powerful for a lot of people. It's an identifying universe and something that creates a community. Anything that does that can heal people. You can have that thing in common and find others. I don't know that it saves lives, but I do know it improves them. ☙

STAR WARS: THE LAST JEDI

ESSENTIAL TRIVIA

Luke Skywalker uses Sheev Palpatine's Sith name, Darth Sidious, for the first time.

The Canto Bight sequence includes a long tracking shot that was inspired by a similar shot from the 1927 film, *Wings*.

Finn and Rose are accused of violating parking regulation 27B/6. This was also the name of a form that appears in Terry Gilliam's 1985 film, *Brazil.*

The Last Jedi features a large number of cameo appearences, including: Joseph Gordon-Levitt, Justin Theroux, Gareth Edwards, Joe Cornish, Michaela Coel, Lily Cole, and Adrian Edmondson. Royal princes William and Harry had non-speaking roles as stormtroopers, but their scenes were cut.

Not just a Jedi Master, Mark Hamill also voices the part of Dobbu Scay, the character who mistakes BB-8 for a slot machine.

The main Resistance cruiser is named the *Raddus* after the Mon Calamari Admiral who appeared in *Rogue One: A Star Wars Story.*

Rian Johnson included a reference to the first *Star Wars* fan film, *Hardware Wars* (1978), with a scene involving an iron.

Every *Star Wars* film includes a character saying, "I've got a bad feeling about this." In *The Last Jedi*, BB-8 says the line in his own droid language.

The hyperspace tracking technology that the First Order use to chase down the Resistance is first alluded to in *Rogue One: A Star Wars Story.*

Mark Hamill's three children, Nathan, Griffin, and Chelsea appear as Resistance fighters on Crait.

On Ahch-To, the door to Luke's hut is a reclaimed wing from his X-wing starfighter.

The film is dedicated to the memory of Carrie Fisher who passed away on December 27, 2016.

The production name for *The Last Jedi* was "Space Bear."

Damage incurred from the blaster fire on Jabba's sail barge are still visible on Luke's mechanical hand.

You can see Vice Admiral Holdo say "pew" when she fires her stun blast at C'ai Threnalli.

The porg species is not named onscreen.

Rian Johnson has claimed that *The Last Jedi* took influence from *Twelve O'clock High* (1949), *Letter Never Sent* (1960), The *Bridge on the River Kwai* (1957), and *Three Outlaw Samurai* (1964).

The Last Jedi was the first *Star Wars* movie not to feature Peter Mayhew as Chewbacca, with Joonas Suotamo taking over.

Issue #49 of the original run of *Star Wars* comics produced by Marvel in 1981 was called *The Last Jedi.*

The shot of Finn waking up was originally planned to be the first shot of the film following the opening crawl.

The novelization of *The Last Jedi* features a dream sequence in which Luke imagines he is married to Camie and still living on Tatooine.

The phrase "The Last Jedi" appears in the opening crawl of *The Force Awakens*, marking the only occasion the title of a different *Star Wars* film appears in the opening crawl.

The Last Jedi is the first film since the original release of *The Phantom Menace* to feature a puppet version of Yoda.

The three dissolve cuts in the scene when Kylo is considering shooting Leia's ship was a callback to the three dissolve cuts between Luke Skywalker and Darth Vader in *The Empire Strikes Back.*

Rey and Poe Dameron don't actually meet until the very end of the film.

The Last Jedi is the first time since *Return of the Jedi* that we seen a Force spirit. It is also the first time that Yoda's Force spirit speaks.

The Last Jedi is the only *Star Wars* film in which a character says the name of the film. In this case, it's Luke who says the title.

STAR
THE RISE OF SKYWALKER
WARS

The Rise of Skywalker was the movie tasked with not only bringing the sequel trilogy to a close but also marking the final chapter in the Skywalker saga. Returning behind the camera was writer/director J.J. Abrams.

Kathleen Kennedy (President of Lucasfilm): It's amazing to think that back in 1977, George Lucas created something that would still resonate with people today. And so, to think we created the story that basically brings the saga to a conclusion, there was a huge responsibility associated with that.

J.J. Abrams (Writer/Director): As a filmmaker, I needed to bring the movie to a conclusion that it and the fans deserved. *The Rise of Skywalker* is not just the end of three movies, but rather the end of nine movies. There was certainly a lot to consider. Chris Terrio—who wrote the script with me—and I never wanted to forget what makes *Star Wars* potent and resonant and alive. The excitement and the passion Chris has for this story and this world was a constant reminder to me. Chris brought so much to the project; amazement and pure childlike enthusiasm. I couldn't be more grateful or more comforted by the company I was in while making this movie.

Daisy Ridley (Rey): While filming *The Force Awakens,* I was very tense and nervous. But because I worked with J.J. on that movie, our relationship was a bit different this time around. I didn't feel as tense and nervous; I felt very comfortable.

Adam Driver (Kylo Ren): It was great, especially since J.J. and I already had the experience of working on *The Force Awakens* together and got to know one another then. For *The Rise of Skywalker*, we had a meeting early on where we decided that

3 /

1 / Daisy Ridley as Rey, on location in Jordan. (Previous spread)

2 / J.J. Abrams flanked by Oscar Isaac, Michelle Rejwan and R2-D2, meet Klaud.

3 / Oscar Isaac shares a joke with Abrams on location.

4 / Abrams and Joonas Suotamo (Chewbacca) check the script.

any idea, anything that we came up with would be discussed, whether it was good or bad. We didn't want to hold anything back.

John Boyega (Finn): Initially, I didn't connect the script to the Skywalker saga at the moment I was reading it. For me, it was just

the end of our five-year journey, our little contribution to this big story. It felt weird knowing we were going to bring it to a conclusion.

Oscar Isaac (Poe Dameron): It has been such a wild, wild journey. I think back five years ago when I got the call to meet J.J., Kathleen

Kennedy, and Lawrence Kasdan where they pitched me the story about this great character, Poe. He went from dying spectacularly in *The Force Awakens* to surviving and becoming a leader of a resistance. I just begged for my life until J.J. Abrams agreed that I could make it off of Jakku! It's definitely good to be alive.

John Boyega: Thinking back on *The Force Awakens*, you realize everything has led to this moment. It feels nice to be one of the main characters in this story. I mean, wow! It's been a blessing and an honor.

Michelle Rejwan (Producer): It's not just the finale of one film, but rather the finale of a trilogy and the culmination of nine films. There were a lot of storylines coming together and we hoped audiences would find it emotionally satisfying, surprising, thrilling, scary, and unexpected.

▶

4 /

John Boyega: At the conclusion of *The Last Jedi*, the Resistance was at a really low point, having been handily defeated by the First Order. At the start of *The Rise of Skywalker,* their numbers have been greatly reduced and there isn't much hope. What hope the Resistance does have is put into the hands of Rey, Poe, and Finn. And these three have to find a solution to resolve the conflict.

Oscar Isaac: At this point, the Resistance has been decimated, and there's only a small group left. Some time has passed since the events of *The Last Jedi,* which enables the group to get some help, gather a few allies, and recruit some new Resistance fighters. However, despite this, they are still scrambling to find even more help somewhere in the galaxy. Poe and Finn have been on some rather insane missions, desperately trying to find a way to fight back against the First Order. Meanwhile, Rey is with the others continuing her training.

Mark Hamill (Luke Skywalker): I never expected to be back. I thought if they did a third trilogy, it would be set ten, fifty, or even one hundred years in the future, so it was completely unexpected. I enjoyed it in a way I never could have in my twenties.

Kathleen Kennedy: When we made *The Force Awakens,* we had a huge weight on our shoulders to essentially reignite the franchise and reintroduce *Star Wars* to a new generation. And now, to have had everybody coming back and working together, J.J. and a lot of the crew, it was like the family coming back together. We didn't have to go through that initial stage of getting to know people and figuring out how everyone would work together. We felt pretty comfortable with each other. It was really nice to make this movie with that kind of feeling.

Chris Terrio (Co-writer): J.J.'s brain works really fast, it's like a computer, and he never forgets anything. I think this movie has required so much creativity, not to mention mind and heart, that J.J. has been preparing for his whole life, and I feel it shows. He always came onto the set with authority and with a clarity about what he wanted, but also with a good sense of humor. It was so inspiring to see J.J. not only working with the actors, but the whole team. Everyone from the scenic painters to the camera department and props department and down the line. We all wanted to give J.J. our very best effort, all the time.

Daisy Ridley: I just wanted the audience to be happy and fulfilled with the film. J.J. and Chris Terrio did an amazing job crafting the story and tying in all nine episodes. J.J. really wanted to make a great film, and everyone involved with the production was just stellar at their jobs. I found it to be really moving. At the end of the day, if you took away the space element, the *Star Wars* of it all, it's about people and how they make their way in life, confronting and dealing with the difficulties they experience.

Oscar Isaac: There were times J.J. would do one long scene in one take. Sometimes it would be quite complicated, with multiple people in the scene, and he would choreograph the whole thing. And what's wonderful about that as an actor, is that it's up to you to dictate the rhythm. When you shoot a scene all in one take, the actors get to really have some fun, which enables a bit of improvisation. Although J.J. had this incredible task of bringing closure to a saga more than forty years in the making, he still had a looseness about him and a curiosity to try different things. He just had this unrelenting vision about what he wanted to accomplish, not to mention

5 /

incredible energy and drive. That was really exhilarating.

Naomi Ackie (Jannah): J.J. was so open to hearing about ideas and allowed everyone to get involved. And considering how much he had on his shoulders, he was always super calm, he had a great sense of humor, and he really made everyone feel at ease. I had never seen anything like it. He was just incredible.

Joonas Suotamo (Chewbacca): First of all, I was so happy J.J. agreed to come back to direct this movie. Working with him on *The Force Awakens* allowed me to observe and learn from him, which was one of the highlights for me. For this film, I felt like it was another opportunity to learn

5 / Veteran *Star Wars* actor Anthony Daniels suits up again as protocol droid C-3PO!

6 / Poe Dameron, ace pilot and leader of the Resistance.

▶ more from him, to push myself to better portray this character. I also felt this time around he gained a new understanding about how to approach Chewbacca. He was able to more effectively communicate what it was I was supposed to do. Very early on, we found a common beat, which was tremendous.

Kelly Marie Tran (Rose Tico): J.J. has this ability to get the best out of the actors he directs, so it was really awesome to work with him. It was a fun environment.

The movie was co-written by Academy Award-winning writer, Chris Terrio.

Chris Terrio: I came to *Star Wars* as a fan, first and foremost. *Return of the Jedi* was the first film I ever saw, and I made my father drop me off to see it every weekend for, I think, about six months. When it came to this project, I had extremely high expectations —it meant the world to me—and I didn't take the responsibility lightly. There wasn't a day where J.J., Michelle Rejwan, and I weren't in constant communication because we all knew we needed to get it right. Every waking moment was devoted to this movie while we were making it.

Michelle Rejwan: Working with Chris Terrio has been absolutely the greatest fun I've had on a film. [Laughs] He is so unbelievably passionate, smart, and dedicated, and works so incredibly hard. He's just relentless at wanting things to be absolutely right, I mean down to a word. I just love his tenacity, and his passion, and his big heart.

Chris Terrio: There were days we arrived on set and we were utterly shocked by what everyone had been able to do. As it went along, it was a series of continual wonders and astonishments. A small conversation between J.J.,

7 /

Michelle, Kathy [Kennedy] and myself was suddenly realized on a grand scale. It was all accomplished with the help of many people from the creature department, the costume and production designers, and of course by the visual effects team. It's an amazing world they created. It's the conclusion of the Skywalker saga, and it needed to be emotional and exciting and gratifying, as well as surprising and inevitable.

Throughout the process, J.J., Michelle, Kathy and I got to a certain point where we could finish each other's sentences. We were constantly challenging each other all the time to make things better. It was incredibly collaborative. There were times J.J. would push me not to go with my first idea, but to keep going to try and find a better idea. And it's not just production, we were all so collaborative with the various departments—art, creature, and costume. It's a hard thing to say, but you can't really put into words when you see or feel something that is *Star Wars*. You just know it's right, whether in regards to design and story or the emotions of the characters.

For Daisy Ridley, returning as Rey meant training to meet the increasing demands of the role.

Daisy Ridley: Working on the previous movies was exhausting. This time, I wanted to be sure I had enough stamina; I wanted to be healthy and, most importantly, ready. I even started kickboxing.

7 / Oscar Isaac and John Boyega show some camaraderie on set.

8 / Poe Dameron is united with his trusty droid, BB-8.

9 / Second unit director Victoria Mahoney works on a scene with Daisy Ridley.

When it came time to do all the required stunts, I felt I *was* ready for the challenge. Mentally, I had to prepare to do some rather terrifying things, and I had to completely trust the stunt team I was working with. I was doing things I never thought I would be doing, such as being strapped into a harness connected to wires and diving off a thirty-foot-tall platform. But because I trusted the team around me, I felt I could do anything they asked me to.

Kathleen Kennedy: First of all, I give George huge credit for creating Princess Leia, who is certainly one of the greatest female heroes in cinema. He also did that in *Indiana Jones* with Marion. I think introducing Rey

to a whole generation of young girls has been fantastic. It has been fascinating to watch Daisy get into a role like Rey at nineteen or twenty years old and then to watch her mature in the role into her mid-twenties. When she first began, nobody knew who she was, she was just getting started in the business. Even the idea of getting strong physically and being able to handle the stunts and the lightsaber fights was all new to her. And now, she's emerged as a powerful figure in these stories. I think there's an interesting parallel to Daisy and Rey's development that really comes through in the movie.

John Boyega: During these three movies, Daisy has been given

latitude to express herself through Rey, and with *The Rise of Skywalker,* she was able to expand upon her character. Daisy has great instinct as an actor, which is something I noticed during the audition process for *The Force Awakens.*

Oscar Isaac: It's really been great to see Daisy's growth and to see Rey's character evolve. When we first met Rey in *The Force Awakens* she had incredible raw potential. She already had so much power within her, but had yet to discover it. For *The Last Jedi,* it was really about Rey understanding who she was, and desperately searching for answers. And now in *The Rise of Skywalker,* we get to see the culmination of all ▶

▶ of Rey's pain, confusion, and power channeled into this ferocious, incredible character. Daisy's performance is just astounding.

Making his final appearance as Luke Skywalker, Mark Hamill made a brief but significant contribution to the story.

Mark Hamill: *Star Wars* is such a positive film. It is so optimistic, so inspiring. It encourages you to do the right thing, because it's the right thing to not think of yourself, but rather to do what's right for the greater good.

Hamill, a fan of fantastical cinema, still has a passion for acting in movies over forty years after the original *Star Wars* film.

Mark Hamill: I was one of those kids who read the *Famous Monsters* magazines, which I loved. I loved the Universal horror films and the Hammer films. Fantasy in general. *King Kong* (1933), the black-and-white movie directed by Willis O'Brien, was my favorite. If you told nine-year-old me I would be making movies, I wouldn't have believed you. I'm so lucky to love what I do and to still be able to keep doing it.

The film presents a turning point for Kylo Ren as he chooses between the dark side and the light.

Adam Driver: To step back a moment, when J.J. and I first met, he told me to imagine a journey for Kylo that was opposite of Darth Vader. Whereas Vader is very confident when the audience first meets him, over the course of three movies, he is chipped away at until he's at his most vulnerable. Kylo's journey is almost the complete opposite. He starts out very vulnerable, very child-like, and then over time, he gains experience and becomes hardened and more assured about the choices he makes. The journey Kylo went through really opened up my imagination as an actor.

10 / The crew of the *Millennium Falcon* engage in some lightspeed skipping to escape the First Order.

11 / Maz Kanata joins the Resistance effort.

Kathleen Kennedy: From a character standpoint, the relationship between Rey and Kylo Ren really drives the story in this particular saga, and I think it's hugely emotional. It was interesting to watch Daisy and Adam delve into exactly what their characters' relationship meant to the two of them.

After surviving against the odds, Poe Dameron, played by Oscar Isaac, returned to lead the effort against the First Order.
Oscar Isaac: In *The Rise of Skywalker*, J.J. really wanted the audience to get to know Poe. Not only that, but to see what he would be like when he's working with a group, and not just by himself. It was just so energizing and so much fun for me as an actor because there was a lot of room for improvisation.

Daisy Ridley: It was really fun. In a lot of ways because I hadn't properly worked with Oscar before. Previously, we had only

shot two tiny scenes together. In *The Rise of Skywalker*, one of our first scenes shows us arguing. J.J. told us our relationship had grown 'off-screen,' since there was a year or so in between the events of *The Last Jedi* and this movie. So, there's a chemistry fostered "in between" the movies. And then John [Boyega] is just amazing.

Oscar Isaac: Poe finds himself inheriting a Resistance that is on the brink of collapse. He feels completely lost, and he even begins to wonder if there's really anything to lead at this point. But Poe is reminded about family and friends and not being alone. And he rallies behind those ideas and pushes the others to continue to move forward.

In his role as the former stormtrooper FN-2187, otherwise known as Finn, John Boyega has been at the forefront of the action. *The Rise of Skywalker* saw the character finding his place as a part of the team.

John Boyega: I definitely wanted Finn to eventually find his place, to be part of a team he's not only fighting for but rooting for as well. I wanted Finn to become strong and not have his strength always questioned. I wanted to show his growth and to show he has an understanding of his world and the people around him, as well as his past.

Oscar Isaac: In as much as these movies are about the Skywalker saga, for me, doing these movies has also been the saga of me meeting John Boyega and to experience this adventure with him. He has such a beautiful heart and is such a beautiful person. I definitely admire him. My first screen test back on *The Force Awakens* was with John, in the TIE fighter. And we've been back-to-back ever since. The exciting thing about *The Rise of Skywalker* is John and I get a ▶

chance to really work together, to interact with one another and have fun. And the reason it *was* so fun to work on this movie is that he and I got do so much together. I just love him.

J.J. put the trio together, and I think it definitely helped capture some of the spirit from the original trilogy. There's a dynamic between the three main characters that's really great.

The Rise of Skywalker also features the return of a promoted Rose Tico.

Kelly Marie Tran: The Resistance is always taking a beating from the First Order. Everything is pretty dire. In *The Last Jedi*, Rose was so full of hope. So from that standpoint, I don't feel she's the same person. But her role has also changed in this movie. She went from being this mechanic to working her way up in the Resistance to having more of a leadership position.

The actress was pleased to be reunited with John Boyega.

Kelly Marie Tran: John Boyega is one of my favorite people, so it was great to work with him again. He's someone who I really look up to, especially in terms of seeing how he took everything in his stride. And it was really cool to work with the cast and crew who were on the last movie too—I felt like I was coming home. The entire experience was really special.

The Rise of Skywalker saw the cast clad in some bold new costumes, courtesy of costume designer Michael Kaplan.

John Boyega: Michael did a great job. This time around, Finn has his own thing going, you know? A new style. He basically went to the Resistance beauty camp. He's now color-coordinating: blue and brown pants, brown waistcoat. He has new hair. I mean, in the stress of war, why not look good fighting?

12 /

Daisy Ridley: For the most part, the costumes have been very similar: they're all meant to be utilitarian, using earthy colors. For *The Force Awakens*, it took a long time to establish the look, but that wasn't the case this time around. For this movie, my costume is pretty much white, which was great because we were filming in the sun. It just looks gorgeous. As for the hair, the team went for something that looked slightly different than before, but still retained the same silhouette. My makeup pretty much stayed the same—all natural.

Keri Russell (Zorii Bliss): My costume is the coolest one I've ever worn! It has this helmet that I really loved wearing, because there was such a power to wearing it. There's something in being hidden that innately gives you this other kind of strength. It's very unnerving to people when they can't see you, but you can see them. And because you can't see my eyes, you don't know what I'm thinking. J.J. wanted

Zorii to be alluring, to keep the audience wondering about who she is. I really loved that. Also, she's a badass, and I really liked that as well.

A new droid joined the cast for this film, the timid D-O.

Oscar Isaac: BB-8 finds himself as the surrogate father to this little droid, D-O. This is another nod by J.J. and Chris to capture some of that spirit from the original trilogy. D-O's just so goshdarn cute and a really fun addition to the *Star Wars* galaxy.

The movie also featured the return of an old favorite, Billy Dee Williams, back in the cape as Lando Calrissian.

Billy Dee Williams (Lando Calrissian): I had no reservations whatsoever [about coming back]. At times, I wondered if Lando would return. So I was very happy about being asked to come back.

12 / The heroes face danger under the sands of Pasaana.

13 / Finn mans the *Millennium Falcon's* guns as the First Order closes in.

14 / Rose Tico and Rey plan their next move.

Daisy Ridley: Billy Dee, who's such a suave man, brought so much joy to the set. It's great he came back for this movie. There was a particular scene where the rest of us were so exhausted, yet he just kept going! He didn't need any rest or anything. And his overall vibe was just great. He was showing me pictures of his granddaughter one day and told me I reminded him of her. I thought that was really sweet.

Billy Dee Williams: When I wore the cape for the first time, I made it very much a part of Lando's persona. I mean, Lando has style. There's no doubt about it.

John Boyega: That was cool. It was good to see Lando back, and it was good to work with Billy. We all knew when he was going to be on set the first time. I even dressed up in a specific way, coordinating to go with his style, just in case he wanted to take a picture. He's the most suave man in the galaxy, with his yellow shirt and cape. I mean, he has a cape—and he doesn't even fly! I want a cape!

Billy Dee Williams: I don't take myself too seriously. I mean, I do take my work seriously, but I don't take myself seriously. Vulnerability is very much a part of who I am.

Naomi Ackie: Being on set and acting with Billy Dee Williams was great. Lando Calrissian is, hands down, one of the coolest characters in the whole world.

Daisy Ridley: I found working with Naomi and Keri really lovely. Naomi did a scene with Billy Dee, and my dad was in the same scene as a pilot. I went onset to watch them film it and he's literally right behind them—classic! And then Keri was just really awesome. Her character is really cool— she's such a badass.

Joonas Suotamo: I had met Billy a few times before this movie. He's just such a friendly, honorable man. It was great to have him sit beside me in the *Millennium Falcon* and act alongside him. He gave me lots of good advice. I'll be grateful forever to him.

Billy Dee Williams: J.J. Abrams is so imaginative, and so much fun to work with. Making *The Rise of Skywalker* has been one of the high points of my career.

One of the highlights of the movie was the epic lightsaber battle atop the wreckage of the destroyed second Death Star.

Adam Driver: A lot of it pretty much evolved while we were working on it. The battle was really physically exhausting, but at the same time very exciting. We were wet and soaked and cold and on wires. I loved it. ▶

13 /

14 /

▶ **Daisy Ridley:** Physically, the lightsaber fight with Adam Driver on the wreckage of the Death Star was tough. What made it more challenging than the other lightsaber fights was that we were being doused with water cannons the whole time. And since it was November in England, it was very cold as well.

Adam Driver: We were fighting on a really slippery, uneven bridge with huge cannons shooting water at us. We were absolutely exhausted at the end of it.

The lightsaber fight on the Death Star wasn't the only action sequence that proved to be a challenge for the actors.

Daisy Ridley: As far as just being the most challenging scene, it had to have been working atop the speeders while filming in Jordan. The vehicle we were riding on was tilted a certain way, which really made my knees hurt by the end of the day. And because we had wind machines constantly going, a piece of sand scratched my eye, causing it to become puffy and irritated. It's weird because technically we didn't

15 / Adam Driver and J.J. Abrams confer on the wrecked Death Star II set.

16 / Billy Dee Williams returns as General Lando Calrissian.

17 / Naomi Ackie as the former stormtrooper, Jannah.

18 / Chewbacca and Rey give chase across the sands of Pasaana.

really look like we were doing anything. It took many hours working on a moving vehicle, which made it tough.

Emerging from the underworld on the frigid world of Kijimi, Zorii Bliss, played by Keri Russell, is an unlikely ally.

Keri Russell: She kind of lives in the gray area between right and wrong. She's done some rather sketchy things in her lifetime and she has a tough exterior—she's very much a survivor.

Oscar Isaac: Keri had such a presence on set. She's small and slender, but she has so much power as a performer. And her voice is incredible.

Keri Russell: I have three kids. And even though I've been an actor for a long time, there is nothing else I have ever done where my son thought it was cool. He said, "Wow!" And what I love about these movie is the metaphor of "believing in yourself." It's a good message.

A deserter from the First Order, Jannah plays a key role in toppling Emperor Palpatine's Final Order.

Naomi Ackie: Jannah is the leader of a group of vagabonds who live on a junk world. They are all just surviving the best way they know how while trying to avoid being discovered by the First Order. And even though she's a strong, capable leader, she also has a vulnerability about

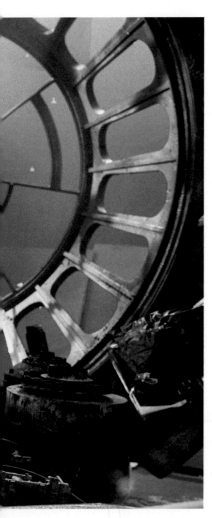

I'm from East London and there aren't any horses around there. I was just really taken by how large, powerful, and beautiful horses are! And yeah—I'm now an equestrian! I feel very at home on a horse after this experience, and it's a new skill I have that I most definitely did not have before.

As well as being proficient with her steed, Jannah is also skilled when it comes to armed combat.

Naomi Ackie: Jannah has the coolest bow and arrow I have ever seen. It's not only awesome, but deadly. It's a two-handed weapon that she can swing from one side to the other. She's a very resourceful person, by the way. She actually made her own arrows out of old material and whatever else she could find in her environment.

17 /

her, an insecurity. But at the end of the day, she is fighting for a cause, a greater good, that drives her, which ultimately overrides her vulnerabilities and insecurities.

The role required Ackie to take to horseback, which led to the actress picking up some new equestrian skills.

Naomi Ackie: Jannah has a trusty steed called an orbak—it's a four-legged creature and very furry. To prepare for the role meant months of training on horseback, which I've now become very adept at. I can ride using one hand, no hands, and shoot a bow and arrow while doing it! When I started the journey, I was terrified of horses as I had never seen one up close.

Making his fourth appearance as Chewbacca, Joonas Suotamo returns as the mighty Wookiee.

Joonas Suotamo: To me, Chewie has always resembled the epitome of loyalty and friendship. When it comes down to it, he is a very stable, trustworthy companion. He continually proves himself through his courageous actions. He's always there doing the right thing.

Suotamo was required to wear the furry suit for filming, often in uncomfortably hot conditions such as the desert in Jordan.

Joonas Suotamo: The first day was a cruel wake-up call. The sun was scorching, and I was holding onto an umbrella to shield myself. It got better as my body became climatized. It really helped that I was wearing a cool shirt underneath my suit that circulated cold water around my torso.

During filming, the crew was always concerned with whether I was getting too hot or too uncomfortable. Depending on how much time we had in between takes, it was usually just easier to stay in the suit. It came down to mind over matter. ▶

18 /

▶ The actor, who had recently become a father when the film was shot, was delighted to welcome his son on set.

Joonas Suotamo: My son saw me in the suit for the first time. He wasn't afraid. He heard my voice underneath the mask, and I lifted him up for everyone to see. I even have a picture of the two of us together. To have my son there on set was one of the greatest moments of my life.

The conclusion of the Skywalker saga ends marks the end of a nine-film, forty-two year saga that has captured the imagination of generations of audiences.

Oscar Isaac: What J.J. and Chris did for this movie was a monumental task. They found a way to encompass the Skywalker saga in a meaningful way to make it feel both surprising and inevitable. When I first read the

script, I was pretty emotional because there was a finality to it, and it's hard to image *Star Wars* could ever have that. One of the most amazing things about the *Star Wars* galaxy, which is what George Lucas did from the very get-go, was to make it feel like there were events happening outside of the movies. Every prop and every character had its own history, and the movies just showed us a glimpse of those things. He allowed people to open up their imaginations and wonder what happened before. I think the mystery of it all also helped to create the phenomenon *Star Wars* is today. And so to take all that, to capture that spirit, and bring it to a conclusion was such an amazing task. I think J.J. and Chris did an incredible job. To go from *A New Hope* and get to where we are with *The Rise of Skywalker* is astounding.

John Boyega: *Star Wars* has been such a major part of my life these last few years. And it wasn't until I got a role in *Star Wars* that my life changed, rapidly, at an amazing speed, and it's been great. And for me, what has stood out the most, what is the most heartwarming, is the collaboration I've shared with all the amazing individuals who have

19 / Joonas Suotamo holds his son aloft on set.

20 / Palpatine makes his evil presence felt.

21 / J.J. Abrams directs *Star Wars'* longest serving actor, Anthony Daniels.

been a part of creating these movies. I've made friends and become part of a big family, and that's a major thing to let go of. As for Finn, I feel good about him. He went from being part of something oppressive to being thought of as a hero.

Oscar Isaac: I was surprised by the passion of the fans and how it never waivers. Throughout the years, I have attended things like Celebration, D23, and comic-cons, and I have seen how much *Star Wars* means to people, and how parents have passed along that passion to their kids. I am also surprised that I am a real part of the lineage and history of these films. And it's not just these movies: there is a long, beautiful history during these last forty-plus years. It's more than a movie, it's a cultural phenomenon. To have been part of telling the story, and not only telling the story, but to be part of its conclusion, has been completely fulfilling and so profound.

Daisy Ridley: It's a very worthy ending. J.J. and co-writer Chris Terrio are so knowledgeable about *Star Wars*, and they are both huge fans as well. Everyone felt good about what we were

doing, and we all had a genuine feeling of joy about what we accomplished. I think that carried over onto the screen.

Mark Hamill: Wherever I go, people are so warm and so friendly. It's quite amazing. Of course, not only do they watch the films repeatedly, but they read the novels and the comic books, and they play the videogames and the role-playing games—all of it. I understand it's not for everybody, but the people who do like it, absolutely love it with a passion that is just indescribable.

For one cast member, *The Rise of Skywalker* marked the end of a personal journey, being the only person to appear in all nine movies.

Anthony Daniels (C-3PO): It was great to see C-3PO have real purpose, to be very involved and part of a team. On my final day of shooting, it was very moving, a very bittersweet moment. Making these movies has been hard work, but it has also been fun and a great joy for me. I have been in *Star Wars* since day one out in Tunisia in 1976, so it has been quite something to have survived this long. It really has been quite a ride. ☺

STAR WARS
THE RISE OF SKYWALKER

DECEMBER 20

STAR WARS: THE RISE OF SKYWALKER

ESSENTIAL TRIVIA

The opening crawl begins with the line, "The dead speak!" An exclamation point has only appeared in one other opening crawl: *Revenge of the Sith*.

Creative rounding by Finn states that Chewbacca is 250 years old.

A new Force ability features in the film. Rey uses the Force to heal a sand serpent and, later, Kylo Ren. The Child has similar abilities in *The Mandalorian*.

The revived Palpatine tells Kylo Ren: "The dark side of the Force is a pathway to many abilities some consider to be unnatural." This is word for word what he tells Anakin Skywalker in *Revenge of the Sith*.

The film features a brief cameo from Denis Lawson as Wedge Antilles. The character last appeared in *Return of the Jedi* thirty-six years ago. *The Rise of Skywalker* is the first time his full name has appeared in the credits.

The Rise of Skywalker contains cameo appearances from Dhani Harrison, Nigel Godrich, and JD Dillard as stormtroopers. Karl Urban, who was directed by J.J. Abrams in two *Star Trek* films, plays the stormtrooper who says, "Knights of Ren" as the warriors walk past.

Ed Sheeran and Lin-Manuel Miranda play members of the Resistance, though Sheeran is largely unrecognizable due to a slip-on mask.

Daisy Ridley's dad, Christopher, appears as a member of the Resistance during the final celebration scenes.

Star Wars composer John Williams makes his debut in front of the camera as Oma Tres—an anagram of "maestro"—a bartender on Kijimi. Kevin Smith can also be found walking the streets of the snowy planet.

Mark Hamill lends his vocal talents to play Boolio, the horned alien who drops the hint about a mole in the First Order.

Sir Alec Guinness's granddaughter, Sally Guinness, plays a First Order officer on the Supreme Council.

A Clone Wars-era battle droid can be seen in Babu Frik's workshop.

J.J. Abrams is one of only two people to direct more than one *Star Wars* film, the other being George Lucas!

The working title for *The Rise of Skywalker* was "TrIXie."

J.J. Abrams provided the voice for the droid D-O, while writer Chris Terrio voiced Aftab Ackbar, the son of Admiral Ackbar.

Maz Kanata was brought to life with an animatronic model, unlike in the previous films where she was created using CGI.

The sequel trilogy was the first time a *Star Wars* trilogy of films saw release in the same decade.

The brief flashback showing Luke and Leia training was filmed using Carrie Fisher's daughter, Billie Lourd, as a stand-in for her mother.

Warwick Davis reprises his role as Wicket at the end of the movie. He is joined on screen by his real life son, Harrison.

Rey's mother is played by *Killing Eve* (2018 – present) star, Jodie Comer.

The Jedi voices at the climax of the film are: Mark Hamill as Luke Skywalker (*A New Hope, The Empire Strikes Back, Return of the Jedi, The Force Awakens, The Last Jedi*), Hayden Christensen as Anakin Skywalker (*Attack of the Clones, Revenge of the Sith, Return of the Jedi*), Olivia D'Abo as Luminara Unduli (*The Clone Wars*), Ashley Eckstein as Ahsoka Tano (*The Clone Wars, Rebels*), Jennifer Hale as Aayla Secura (*The Clone Wars*), Samuel L. Jackson as Mace Windu (*The Phantom Menace, Attack of the Clones, Revenge of the Sith*), Ewan McGregor (*The Phantom Menace, Attack of the Clones, Revenge of the Sith*) and Alec Guinness (*A New Hope, The Empire Strikes Back, Return of the Jedi*) as Obi-Wan Kenobi, Frank Oz as Yoda (*The Phantom Menace, Attack of the Clones, Revenge of the Sith, The Empire Strikes Back, Return of the Jedi, The Last Jedi*), Angelique Perrin as Adi Gallia (*The Clone Wars*), Freddie Prinze Jr. as Kanan Jarrus (*Rebels*), and Liam Neeson as Qui-Gon Jinn (*The Phantom Menace, The Clone Wars*).

STAR WARS LIBRARY

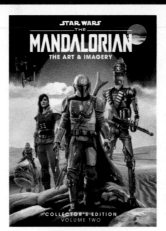

STAR WARS: THE EMPIRE STRIKES BACK: THE OFFICIAL COLLECTOR'S EDITION

THE MANDALORIAN THE ART AND IMAGERY VOLUME 2

STAR WARS: AGE OF RESISTANCE: THE OFFICIAL COLLECTOR'S EDITION

STAR WARS: THE SKYWALKER SAGA THE OFFICIAL MOVIE COMPANION

- *ROGUE ONE: A STAR WARS STORY* THE OFFICIAL COLLECTOR'S EDITION
- *ROGUE ONE: A STAR WARS STORY* THE OFFICIAL MISSION DEBRIEF
- *STAR WARS: THE LAST JEDI* THE OFFICIAL COLLECTOR'S EDITION
- *STAR WARS: THE LAST JEDI* THE OFFICIAL MOVIE COMPANION
- *STAR WARS: THE LAST JEDI* THE ULTIMATE GUIDE

- *SOLO: A STAR WARS STORY* THE OFFICIAL COLLECTOR'S EDITION
- *SOLO: A STAR WARS STORY* THE ULTIMATE GUIDE
- *THE BEST OF STAR WARS INSIDER* VOLUME 1
- *THE BEST OF STAR WARS INSIDER* VOLUME 2
- *THE BEST OF STAR WARS INSIDER* VOLUME 3
- *THE BEST OF STAR WARS INSIDER* VOLUME 4
- *STAR WARS:* LORDS OF THE SITH
- *STAR WARS:* HEROES OF THE FORCE

- *STAR WARS:* ICONS OF THE GALAXY
- *STAR WARS:* THE SAGA BEGINS
- *STAR WARS* THE ORIGINAL TRILOGY
- *STAR WARS:* ROGUES, SCOUNDRELS, AND BOUNTY HUNTERS
- *STAR WARS* CREATURES, ALIENS, AND DROIDS
- *STAR WARS: THE RISE OF SKYWALKER* THE OFFICIAL COLLECTOR'S EDITION
- *THE MANDALORIAN* THE ART AND IMAGERY VOLUME 1

- *THE MANDALORIAN* THE ART AND IMAGERY VOLUME 2
- *STAR WARS: THE EMPIRE STRIKES BACK* THE 40TH ANNIVERSARY COLLECTOR'S EDITION
- *STAR WARS: AGE OF RESISTANCE* THE OFFICIAL COLLECTOR'S EDITION
- *STAR WARS: THE SKYWALKER SAGA* THE OFFICIAL COLLECTOR'S EDITION

MARVEL LIBRARY

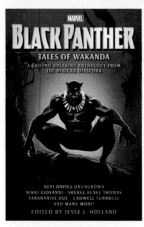

BLACK PANTHER TALES OF WAKANDA

MARVEL STUDIOS' THE COMPLETE AVENGERS

MARVEL STUDIOS' BLACK WIDOW

MARVEL: THE FIRST 80 YEARS

MARVEL CLASSIC NOVELS
- **WOLVERINE** WEAPON X OMNIBUS
- **SPIDER-MAN** THE DARKEST HOURS OMNIBUS
- **SPIDER-MAN** THE VENOM FACTOR OMNIBUS
- **X-MEN AND THE AVENGERS** GAMMA QUEST OMNIBUS
- **X-MEN** MUTANT FACTOR OMNIBUS

NOVELS
- **SPIDER-MAN** MILES MORALES WINGS OF FURY
- **MORBIUS** THE LIVING VAMPIRE: BLOOD TIES
- **ANT-MAN** NATURAL ENEMY
- **AVENGERS** EVERYBODY WANTS TO RULE THE WORLD
- **AVENGERS** INFINITY
- **BLACK PANTHER** WHO IS THE BLACK PANTHER?

- **CAPTAIN AMERICA** DARK DESIGNS
- **CAPTAIN MARVEL** LIBERATION RUN
- **CIVIL WAR**
- **DEADPOOL** PAWS
- **SPIDER-MAN** FOREVER YOUNG
- **SPIDER-MAN** KRAVEN'S LAST HUNT
- **THANOS** DEATH SENTENCE
- **VENOM** LETHAL PROTECTOR
- **X-MEN** DAYS OF FUTURE PAST
- **X-MEN** THE DARK PHOENIX SAGA
- **SPIDER-MAN** HOSTILE TAKEOVER

ART BOOKS
- **MARVEL'S *SPIDER-MAN MILES MORALES* THE ART OF THE GAME**
- **MARVEL'S *AVENGERS* THE ART OF THE GAME**

- **MARVEL'S *SPIDER-MAN* THE ART OF THE GAME**
- **MARVEL *CONTEST OF CHAMPIONS* THE ART OF THE BATTLEREALM**
- *SPIDER-MAN: INTO THE SPIDER-VERSE:* THE ART OF THE MOVIE
- **THE ART OF IRON MAN** 10TH ANNIVERSARY EDITION

MOVIE SPECIALS
- **MARVEL STUDIOS'** *SPIDER-MAN FAR FROM HOME*
- **MARVEL STUDIOS'** *ANT MAN & THE WASP*
- **MARVEL STUDIOS'** *AVENGERS: ENDGAME*
- **MARVEL STUDIOS'** *AVENGERS: INFINITY WAR*
- **MARVEL STUDIOS'** *BLACK PANTHER* (COMPANION)

- **MARVEL STUDIOS'** *BLACK WIDOW*
- **MARVEL STUDIOS'** *CAPTAIN MARVEL*
- **MARVEL STUDIOS'** *SPIDER-MAN: FAR FROM HOME*
- **MARVEL STUDIOS: THE FIRST TEN YEARS**
- **MARVEL STUDIOS'** *THOR: RAGNAROK*

- *SPIDER-MAN: INTO THE SPIDER-VERSE*